The Happy Ever After

A GUIDE TO A FULFILLING RETIREMENT

John J. Navin

John Navin & Associates Inc.
BRENTWOOD, TENNESSEE

John J. Navin/John Navin & Associates Inc.
9019 Overlook Blvd. Suite C1-B
Brentwood, TN 37027
www.johnnavin.com

Book layout ©2013 BookDesignTemplates.com

The Happy Ever After/ John J. Navin. —1st ed.
ISBN 978-1541139688

Contents

Ironman:
What's Your Turning Point?

Julie Moss was dehydrated, tired, burned out and could barely move. Her body was saying, "No more." Yet, somehow, this athlete found the strength to walk toward the finish line during the 1982 Ironman competition. Just 30 yards from the finish line, Kathleen McCartney passed her. Millions of Americans watched mesmerized, as Julie Moss never gave up — never gave up! — and crawled across the finish line in the dark.

Thirty-one years after she crossed the finish line, Julie Moss looked back on the event as a turning point in her life.

"It took all my focus just to keep my body working," she told Ironman.com. "The image was that I was pretty out of it, but it was taking all my focus just to keep going. I had to concentrate so much on how I placed my foot on the ground. If I was off by a bit, my leg would just buckle."

The Ironman consists of a 2.4-mile swim, a 112-mile bicycle ride and a marathon of 26.2 miles. It is considered one of the most difficult one-day sporting events in the world. Without proper training, there is risk of death. The Ironman requires tremendous preparation and sacrifice. It takes a minimum of 13 hours of training per week for half a year to get in shape for an Ironman race. Some of the most successful participants train for over a year.

Julie Moss said the moment when she crossed the finish line was a defining moment in her life. "Everyone has a defining moment, mine just got captured on film," she told Ironman.com. "Every time the tape's played, it hits this deep emotional chord that says I discovered something new about myself on that day, and other people get to see it."

The story of Julie Moss helps us illustrate the possibility of human achievement. She is a metaphor for endurance. She teaches us that no matter how difficult the task or goal, we should carry on, and never give up. Sometimes success is only 30 yards away.

Thousands of people who saw her on ABC Wide World of Sports cite her as the reason they wanted to try out for a triathlon. I — John Navin — was one of them.

When I started training, I learned how hard it was to become an Ironman. I became part of a community of people who are training for the Ironman. This community supports me and holds me accountable. During training season, we train every weekend and several times a week. I get up at 4 a.m. to swim two miles. I bicycle 100 miles with my wife. I adhere to a very strict diet.

Before my first Ironman, I shed 60 pounds. I gave up some of my favorite foods and trained constantly. I completed my first Ironman in 2011.

Crossing the finish line takes tremendous discipline, sacrifice, dedication, persistence, hard work and a never-give-up attitude. These virtues are the winning ways for all sorts of things in life. These are critical values for building wealth for retirement. Most people don't inherit a million dollars for retirement. They have to earn it, save it, grow it and add money to the nest egg with every paycheck. Good savers have a plan; they stick with the plan regardless of the ups and downs in the stock market. This requires discipline, patience and a long-term view.

Julie Moss said her first Ironman was a turning point in her life. People who have saved enough money for retirement are also at a turning point. They don't want to lose what they have saved. They have finished with one race and will be starting a new race. Just as Julie Moss did not give up and crawled across the finish line, good savers did not give up when times were tough. They continued to work, they continued to save. Now those near-retirees are looking at how to achieve a successful retirement without running out of money.

> "When the student is ready, the teacher will appear." — Buddha Siddhartha Gautama (Shakyamuni)

This book contains timeless advice that comes from scholars who have worked on these issues since the dawn of time. Some of the authors and business people who have shaped my thinking are Napoleon Hill, author of "Think And Grow Rich," Dale Carnegie, author of "How To Win Friends and Influence People," Warren Buffett, chairman and CEO of Berkshire Hathaway, Robin Sharma, author of "The Monk Sold His Ferrari," and Jack Canfield, author of "Chicken Soup for the Soul."

One of my favorite quotes from Napoleon Hill is, "You can be anything you want to be, if only you believe with sufficient conviction and act in accordance with your faith; for whatever the mind can conceive and believe, the mind can achieve."

If you desire financial security, better health and more happiness, then this book is for you. This is your instruction manual for how to turn the raw materials of that desire into a solid, structured life — a life you can continually improve and that you're proud to say you live.

Read this book with a yellow marker or pen. Mark or underscore the parts that you find interesting or valuable. Read each chapter thoroughly, maybe two or three times.

Apply these principles at every possible opportunity. Use this book as working handbook to help you solve problems. As Napoleon Hill said in "Think and Grow Rich," we need to make time to think.

As you move through this book, we will focus on the three areas of your life that, while they're interconnected, all deserve distinct attention. We will start with the Personal Area, where we'll focus on what makes you, you — your likes, dislikes, aptitudes and dreams — because this is going to inform the work we'll do in the Financial and Physical areas.

All three of these areas are connected, and successfully working through this book is going to require paying attention to all three areas. As we move forward, you'll begin to see the connections, but each area has its own specific key points that will help you stay focused as you go through the process. When your Personal, Financial and Physical areas work harmoniously together, there is balance, peace and success. You know that feeling when you have a perfect day, when everything you touch turns to gold: You find a $10 bill in the street, your boss calls you and says she loves your work and wants to give a raise, and your best friend invites you out to dinner.

Using the tools in this book, you will create a plan that is unique to you as an individual. I'm here to give you the insights and shortcuts that I've developed over the past 23 years. I've learned through trial and error what works. I can promise you that your efforts will be worth it. My sincere hope is that you will gain clarity where before you may have felt confusion, and that you will experience success in reaching all of your goals.

~John J. Navin

The following are photos of John after completing his first Ironman triathlon. For the Ironman Wisconsin in 2011, he swam 2.4 miles, biked 112 miles, and ran 26.2 miles. Though the race was exacting and his smile is one of exhaustion, this tremendous personal accomplishment was one that brought him a great deal of peace and balance. In 2016, he completed the Ironman Lake Placid. As you peruse this book, he hopes you will be inspired to find your own motivation and "Happy Ever After."

Achieving Personal Balance

Scott and Susan were wonderful parents who sacrificed immensely to create a better life for their two children. They worked hard at their jobs; they helped their children with homework. On the weekends, they took their son to soccer tournaments and their daughter to dance contests. The parents buried their personal desires to help their children grow. Their children graduated from high school and college and were successful responsible adults.

When Mom and Dad became empty nesters, they were left with a lot of free time. Indeed, retirement was not far away, and they had no idea what they would be doing with all that time. *What's next? What am I supposed to do? What do I want?*

That time is often the first time people look inward and begin to ask what's next. How are we going to live out the rest of our lives? If you have health and you have wealth, it is much easier to work on your happiness. Many of my clients often reach a crossroads where they have to make a decision in order to maintain balance in their lives. They needed someone to point the way. They need a plan for income, a plan for evaluating what they love, a plan to exercise, and a plan to develop harmony in their lives and in their community.

The overall focus of this book, beyond all of the exercises, plans and activities, is that you are working on you. You are the focus of this project. I can't give you an exact timetable for completion of this project, but I want you to give it at least one month of solid, concentrated effort.

"Six hundred and seventy-two hours of inner work to profoundly improve every waking moment of the rest of your life is quite a bargain, don't you think?" wrote Robin Sharma in "The Monk Who Sold His Ferrari." "Investing in yourself is the best investment you will ever make. It will not only improve your life, it will improve the lives of all those around you."

The idea behind "The Happy Ever After" is to help you focus the resources you have right now, so that you can maximize your quality of life without unnecessarily spending a ton of money, exerting a ton of effort or wasting a bunch of time. I've already experienced some of the minefields and roadblocks that come up.

I want you to remember that this is your program. You are creating a well-balanced life for yourself. As you go through this process, don't be afraid to take time where you need it, invest money where you need it, and accept that your progress, while it may not be perfect, is uniquely yours. Your pursuit is a journey, not a destination, so take your time and enjoy the pursuit.

The Turnaround

I'm sure you have heard someone say, "If I would have known that I would have lived this long, I would have taken better care of myself." Countless people crawl into their 60s and die. Their bodies are shot. They can't go on vacation in retirement. The best they can do is hang out at their house, maybe work in the garden. But walk five miles? Are you kidding?

I have a friend who struggled with her weight for 20 years. She was obese. My friend had the body of 62-year-old female even though her actual age was 47. Her heart and lungs had the capacity for a sedentary life only. She got upset with herself and did something about this problem. In 12 months, she lost over 100 pounds through diet and regular exercise. My friend is amazing. She is an inspiration. She hikes regularly up to eight miles in the woods to lose weight, connect with friends and nature and create moments of lasting joy. She is happier today than she has been in years. She learned this valuable lesson: If you have your health, you have everything.

The foundation of any life well lived is being alive and healthy enough to enjoy life. What's money if you can't enjoy it?

One thing I have learned after observing many successful business leaders like Warren Buffett and Dale Carnegie. They established a system of business and stuck with the plan. When they veered from the plan, they made mistakes, but learned from them. Over time the plan amassed amazing results.

The Journal

As a part of this program, I'm going to ask you to start a journal. You can do it however you like — buy a Moleskine Notebook at your local bookstore, get a personal recorder and then transcribe the audio, start a Word document, use the "notes" space in your day planner, write a Facebook status update, send yourself emails or write entries in your Outlook calendar. You could start a blog. Whatever works for you is ultimately the best choice.

One of the greatest Americans to keep a journal was Henry David Thoreau. He kept a journal for 24 years until his death in 1862. His technique was simple. He took field notes during the day, and then transcribed his notes into his journals. The journals were the source for larger creative works and essays. "My journal should be a record of the things that I love," he wrote. "I love nature. I love the landscape because it is so sincere."

You may want to take Thoreau's lead and take "field notes" in this book, underline passages and write your thoughts in the margins. You can use your field notes to write in your journal.

Journaling allows you to express yourself freely without constraint. Don't think about who will read your journal. Instead, focus on what you are feeling and thinking. Put those words down. I know someone who has kept a diary for 34 years. He said journaling helped him realize his potential. He set goals every year and used the diary to chart his progress. When he looks back on his dairy, he is amazed at how far he has come.

In the toughest times of my life, I go back through the notes I took 15 years ago from my coaches. I encourage you to do the same. A journal will automatically provide you with the tools necessary to review old notes quickly and efficiently.

We need people in our life. We were not put here to do things alone. You will find there is success in working with other people and asking for help where you need it.

I am always looking for opportunities to learn how to be a better person, a smarter businessman and a better advisor.

Years ago, I had a sales and business coach who taught me a valuable lesson. I was very gung-ho but very young and convinced that there was just some secret I didn't know yet that, as soon as I found it out, I'd be a perfect businessman.

I said: "I want to do the best that I can for my clients, and I want to learn the best sales tips and techniques so that I can reach as many people as possible."

He said: "OK, you want to improve your sales? You need to go to work on you."

I said: "What?"

He said: "Yes. I'm going need you to go to work on you. It's going to cost you probably about $9,000 dollars, and it's going to take a year."

I said: "Are you kidding me?"

He said: "No. If you want to become better at anything, you have to commit to work on you."

So, in 1999, I went to work on me.

Avoid Threats to Happiness

Three major threats to happiness are regret, guilt and repression. If a person focuses on his regrets, looking back on all his mistakes, he is going to feel horrible. If he combines regret with guilt and repression, the resulting feeling is one of dread and emptiness. So, be kind to yourself. Forget the past. Today is a new day, a clean slate. Let us embrace the day and move in the direction of our goals and dreams.

Surround yourself with people who accept you as you are, regardless. True friends have kind things to say about you, they offer their help when they can, and they provide encouragement and validation. Love is a natural human need for people of all ages. There is a 10-year-old girl who is extremely sensitive and shy. She is also very talented in art, music and crafts. When she is allowed the freedom to create, she will go to the piano and play music. Or she might grab her violin and start playing a piece by Chopin. When validated and praised, she works even harder to please. It's pure joy to watch because she is so delightful, creative and beautiful. But if she doesn't get support or is criticized, she cries and runs to her room. The point of the story is this, if we are loved and supported, we can do great things. That love starts within. We must be kind to ourselves and we must surround ourselves with people who love us and support us.

As you work through "The Happy Ever After," it is very important that you treat yourself like a good friend. If you catch yourself saying harsh, critical things to yourself or even saying them out loud about yourself to others, I want you to stop. Just stop. Take a deep breath, and counter that criticism with something good. Remember thoughts are living things. If our thoughts are negative, we may treat others with the same negativity. We all have pain, agony, regrets and demons, but I choose to focus on whatever is lovely, whatever is true, whatever is divine and of lasting value. This book contains timeless truths that have helped people for thousands of years, but you wouldn't find these truths on the evening news. Crime, war and bloodshed are in the news daily, but I am asking you to turn it off. I'm not asking you to bury your head in the sand when it comes to your community and nation, but this book is about taking your life to the next level.

This book is about doing what you can with what you have right now, regardless of what your past is like or what others will think about you. By befriending yourself, you will be more successful throughout the book, and you will feel more positive about your achievements.

Proven Strategies to Create Balance

We are trying to create a balanced life — balanced physically, financially and personally — while making progress toward our goals, reduce our stress levels and feel more fulfilled and free.

Starting in this simple way, we realize that creating a balanced life isn't that hard. What's making it so hard is that we are trying to force things and rush things, racing around trying to get too much done in a short period of time, multitasking and putting all kinds of small, trivial tasks ahead of the big-picture goal of fulfillment. You can take deliberate, conscious steps to achieve your own unique sense of balance by figuring out who you are, what is most important to you and what a well-balanced life looks like for you.

Set Goals

The difference between a goal and a dream is that a goal is something that's written down. It's something you quantify, and there is a date attached to it. Otherwise, it's just a dream. If it's bouncing around your head and it's going round and round, then that's a dream. I think too often we have a dream, but then something happens. We tell ourselves, "Well, that really wasn't a realistic dream," or "I wasn't supposed to do that anyway." It gets overwhelming, and we think, "It's too hard. I think I'm going to stay right here. I'm not going to grow. I'll just be right here and live with what I got, and it'll all work out."

However, if you can commit something to paper by writing it down, it's a goal. There is no such thing as a bad goal. There might be a bad or unrealistic timeline, but there is not a bad goal. There are going to be obstacles; but with goals, you will overcome those obstacles. Negative thoughts are going to creep into your head that say you can't realize your dream; but with goals you will have specific ways to counter those thoughts.

Your first assignment is to seek answers about who you are at the very center. You might find that some answers surprise you, and you might find that some answers conflict with others. That's OK. Just take an honest and open-minded approach to answering the questions. You'll be referring to them throughout the process, expanding upon the answers, and maybe revising them.

What do you like?
What don't you like?
What aren't you willing to do?
What are you willing to do?

I Live This

I want you to know that this book is not just something I say. It's something I live. It's not just something I'm doing so I can go get something else. What I've discovered over the past 23 years is that this is my purpose, my passion. My calling is to help other people figure out how to live a balanced, fulfilling life so they can do great things on a big scale.

You will also discover as you progress through this book that the most important revelations will come from within. I am definitely here to help you, but this is your journey, unique to you.

What's Inside of You?

"There is no reality except the one contained within us. That is why so many people live such an unreal life. They take the images outside of them for reality and never allow the world within to assert itself," Hermann Hesse wrote.

I love that quote from "Steppenwolf," because it shows why so many people have never found their true self. They are caught up following images in the media. These images may be a complete fantasy or have no bearing on their true reality. Yet people spend hours every day looking at pictures on Facebook or Instagram, even if it means feeling inadequate or insecure or miserable, when they compare themselves to those images.

This section is devoted to discovering who you really are, what your calling is, what your unique ability is, what your talents are and how you can use those things to create a meaningful, rewarding and well-balanced life.

This section may feel a little bit overwhelming, but we will break these big questions down into small, tangible steps. By understanding who you uniquely are, you will feel more alive, more fulfilled, more balanced, more purposeful and more intentional every single day.

Finding Your True Self

It has been said that joy or ultimate happiness comes from doing something that motivates you, drives you, pushes you, and fulfills you. Finding that something may be tough, it may not just "appear."

Thoreau wrote in his journal about what he cared about, what was important to him, what he loved. What do you love? What do you feel called to do? What is your personal why? By "why," I mean, what is important to you about effecting personal changes in your life, and why do you want these changes?

Write down your answers in your journal. Consider what you have written. Then, consider the honesty of your answers, and consider the reasons behind why you answered this way.

Continue writing in your journal about these ideas. You can write a lot right now, or you can write a little and come back to the entry later if you feel you need perspective.

Find Your Unique Ability

It is critical in this process to understand what makes you who you are, and to recognize that who you are really makes a difference. We're all here for a reason. Your reason is different than mine. It's also very, very personal. Your journey in discovering your talent is individualized. No two are the same.

It may be something that you haven't looked at in a long, long time. It didn't hit me until I was in my early 30s when I asked myself for the first time, "What is my unique ability? What am I called to do? What am I meant to do?" Now, each time I ask myself these questions, it evolves. It becomes clearer and clearer the more I peel back that onion.

Out of all the ideas presented in this book, this is definitely the one that we cannot rush through. You should go through this process of self-discovery, and then come back and go through it again. You may find that you need to devote more than one journal entry to discovering what is your specialty?

Have you ever stopped and wondered what you really like to do? Is it being around people? Is it giving to others? Is it sports? Is it music? Is it business? Cooking, reading or Facebooking? What is it you really like to do?

You're going to discover that there are things you like to do, there are things that you're good at and there are areas of expertise. They may not be one in the same. In fact, for many people, they are three different things entirely.

When I was introduced to this exercise and the concept of what do I really like to do, I first did it from a business perspective. I said, "What is it in my business that I like to do, and what is it that I'm good at?" Oftentimes, if it's an area of expertise or something you really love to do, those aren't the same things.

For example, I discovered that in business I was very, very good at keeping track of the money and paying bills, but I didn't love to do it. I was very good or efficient at returning emails, but it wasn't something that I loved to do. You can be really great at washing your car. That doesn't mean you love to do it and would consider it a passion. What I really loved to do was to be working with people, creating strategies and thinking of ideas. That's what really got me excited.

I remember once reading an article about a newspaper reporter on a quest to find happiness. This particular reporter tried various jobs over the years. He left the writing business and tried his hand at real estate. He found out he really didn't like working on weekends showing houses. He tried selling stocks. This was attractive to him because of the potential for high income, but he wasn't any good at selling stocks. So in the end he returned to the work of writing. He discovered that the key to happiness and wealth is to find out what you love to do and do it all the time.

So, what is it that gets you excited? What really gets you jazzed up, something you can do all day long without even thinking about? It doesn't mean that you won't be tired after doing it, but something about it will actually recharge you in a way. This passion that you have will come naturally and effortlessly; it will flow into your life. You may not even think it's a unique ability or talent because you do it so effortlessly and naturally. What is it that comes naturally to you or effortlessly?

There was a 90-year-old retired doctor who had not worked in 20 years yet lived a vibrant and active life. His secret for staying healthy was his willingness to keep on learning. At 90, he bought a new Apple computer, which he used to track his finances and keep up with family and friends in social media. He continued to meet with his friends several times a week at a coffee shop. There they talked about business, politics and medicine.

Janina Krell-Roesch, Ph.D., a research fellow at the Mayo Clinic in Scottsdale, Arizona, recently completed a study that found those aged 70 years and older who used a computer once a week or more were 42 percent less likely to develop memory and thinking problems. Researchers followed 1,929 people age 70 and older who were part of the larger Mayo Clinic Study of Aging in Rochester, Minnesota.[1]

Start by listing the activities that make you feel fully alive and energized. What parts of your day do you really love? What activities just make time fly by? You also might choose to devote some of your journaling to what you're good at and what you're an expert on. Don't discount these entirely, but think about them in the light of what you like about those things.

---

[1] American Academy of Neurology. "Using a computer, social activities tied to reduced risk of memory decline." ScienceDaily. ScienceDaily, March 3, 2016.

Once you discover what it is that you like to do, take it a step further and say it out loud: "This is really what I'm passionate about." Then, write it down.

Bonus Activity: Whom Do Others Think You Are?

If you're having a hard time identifying your strengths or your passion — or even if you're just curious or you're an overachiever — reach out for help from those who know you best. Talk to a few of your closest friends. Ask them what they think your unique ability is.

Oftentimes, it's easier for someone else to see what your unique ability is. Ask them for their insight. Include some of the questions that you answered for yourself in the previous sections. It's as simple as saying, "I'm putting together some thoughts and ideas. I would love your insight. Please share with me some of the things you think that I do very, very well. Please share with me some of the things you think come naturally to me."

You're not doing this as a positive boost. That will be a good side effect of it, by the way, but you're doing this to get their insight into some of the things that you do well, into your natural talents and abilities. Journal about your reaction to those responses. Do those close to you know you well? Are there things they see in you that you don't see in yourself?

Focus On Your Strengths

You are unique. You were made for a purpose. No matter what the particular nature of your spiritual beliefs is, there is no question that you have gifts that nobody else has. If you don't dive deep into those to figure out what they are and then find the time to share them with others, you are robbing yourself from fully experiencing all that life has to offer and robbing the rest of the world from experiencing your gifts.

Many of us have been told, especially in school or in business, "Don't focus on your strengths. Focus on your weaknesses so you can improve yourself."

For example, there is a well-known story about a famous pro golfer who found himself in this exact situation. One of his weaknesses was his sand shot, coming out of sand traps. When he approached his coach about this weakness, the coach said, "OK, let's work on your sand game." But what his coach then instructed him to do was actually quite the opposite.

One of his strengths was his drive. He had a very, very good straight long solid drive, so his coach's approach was to go to work on his drive to make it better. Instead of focusing on weakness — in this case his bunker game — they went to work on his drive, which is one of his strengths.

Well, guess what happened? His drive got better. It got longer, and it got straighter. Did his bunker game get any better? No. It didn't get better at all, but what did happen was that he was in the sand less because his drive got better and he was typically in the fairway.

Let's walk through the same approach in regard to your unique abilities and talents. Focus on your strengths, not on your weaknesses. If we focus on the weaknesses, what's going to happen is that, 20 years from now, we're going to have very strong weaknesses, but they're still going to be weaknesses. You won't have worked on becoming uniquely you. You'll just be a less weak version of what people have told you that you should be.

So, what are your strengths? What activities come naturally to you? Write them down. Then, imagine a scenario, just one, in which you share those strengths with others. What does that look like? Where are you, and who are you with? Write down all the details you can think of. Don't be afraid if it seems silly or unrealistic. All the great athletes, the great musicians and the great talent you're going to find started by showing up and sharing their strengths.

Identify What Comes Effortlessly

All right, so we have identified what we're passionate about and what our strengths are, but how do we translate this into our life? It's all well and good to say, "I'm a human resources manager, but I'm passionate about our decorating." That doesn't give us any idea of how to translate this into leading a fulfilled life wherein we also pay our mortgage and get our kids to school on time.

So, how do we utilize our passions and our strengths in life?

Describe Your Ideal Day

I want you to describe your ideal day. If you could organize your day however you would like it, what would it look like? Some people will say, "I would love to just make pottery all day." "I would love to write poetry all day." "I would love to deal with people all day." I want you to be more detailed than that. When would you wake up? What would you have for breakfast? How would you get to work? Where would you work? What would you be doing? With whom would you be working? What leisure activities would you enjoy? Be specific.

The Beekeeper

Brian Carr is a beekeeper, gardener, lawn care specialist and cyclist. His ideal day is getting up at 4:30 a.m. to meditate, drink coffee and read news on the internet. At daybreak, he checks on his garden and bees and feeds his birds. By 8 a.m. he is on his first job, mowing lawns and trimming bushes. He works quickly and efficiently and gets his work done by 3 p.m. each day. He takes a break, and then goes on a 20-mile bike ride, usually by himself but sometimes with a friend. In the evening, he eats and watches the birds at his feeders. By 8 p.m. he is exhausted and goes to bed. Sometimes he wakes up at midnight to view the moon. He might walk around the garden, lie in his hammock and watch the stars. My friend is not a rich man, nor is he poor. He is content. Many years ago, when he worked for a transportation company, he was a miserable man, overweight from eating fast food and drinking too much. He made a radical change at age 55. He gave up the trucking business. He sold most of his possessions and became a beekeeper and planted a garden. He changed his diet, quit drinking, exercised and lost weight. He simplified his life to focus on what really mattered to him: His passions for gardening and cycling. Brian is an incredible cyclist; he bicycles up to 100 miles in a day, no problem. He bicycled across Iowa in Ragbrai, he bicycled across Kansas. Now he is considering bicycling across Africa.

Break the Cycle

It often seems easier and safer to stay in the same place. It seems easier to say, "I'm just going to stay where I am and keep doing what I'm doing because I know what I'm doing."

But this is not, I promise, the path to a balance, fulfilled and happy life.

A few years ago, my brother called me. He had been fired from a job that he hadn't really liked, and he was frustrated. He was hurt, a little scared, and feeling really lost. He was not sure where to turn. I asked, "What are you going to do now?" He said, "Well, I don't know. There are so many possibilities." I asked, "Since you have a few moments, will you take some time to go do a little exercise for yourself?" He said, "All right. What is it?" I talked to him about finding his passion, doing something he really loves to do.

I don't know if he took the time to answer those big-picture questions, but I do know that some important commitments needed his attention, such as his family, his mortgage and his retirement. He got another job relatively quickly doing the same thing as before. He's back to the grindstone, and, in some ways, he is lucky. He is meeting his commitments, which is more than some people can say. But nothing has really changed for him. He just keeps pressing on doing the same thing.

I don't think he took my advice. However, I trust that you will. Taking the time to work on these big questions step-by-step will prepare you to break the cycle of staying where you are just because it's familiar. We all have a natural tendency to flow back into where we came from because we're comfortable with it. We know it, and it's easy.

The task before you now is to get comfortable with your passion. Get comfortable with who you are, what you want and what you have to give. Then, you'll already be working on your balanced life when a game-changing opportunity comes along, even if it's disguised as misfortune.

Take time now to break that cycle. Break the cycle to get yourself on the right track toward a balanced, fulfilling life rather than continuing in your comfort zone of past habits.

Get Off the Treadmill

For most of us, our average day is a hustle and bustle. We're out of time, we're behind schedule, and we're just busy, busy people.

But, if we're going to step back and ask, "What is my unique ability? What is my natural calling? What is my passion?" then we have to get away from some of the busyness in our lives.

If not, we're just stuck on this treadmill. We're never going to have time to step back to take a look, or we're going to think, "Oh, my gosh. I don't have time for that right now. It's really not that important. I've got all these things going on in my life. I can get to it later."

And what we do is excuse it away.

Right now you need to make a commitment to get off the treadmill. Even if it's just once today and you don't know when you can again, start where you can with the idea being to make your goal an hour a week. You need to block off some time on a regular, consistent basis to devote to getting off that never-ending treadmill.

At first it might not seem like it's useful. In fact, it might seem wasteful, but it's tried and true. Many executives and experts in different industries, when asked, "What is your biggest key to success?" will say that they step back. They get out of their business, and they get out of their personal life. They get off the treadmill they're on, and they go sit for just an hour.

When you carve out this time for yourself, unplug the radio, the TV, the clocks or whatever it is that could possibly distract you. Turn your phone off. Shut your computer down. Find a quiet space. Whatever works for you will be fine — nature, your couch, your car, your bathroom. Someplace where you can't be interrupted. What I'd like you to do is just to sit there and try to totally unplug.

The Value of Meditation

Here's what's going to happen, though, at first. During the first 15 minutes, you'll sit there, and you'll say, "This is the stupidest thing I've ever done. Why would John want me to go and sit in this place when there's nobody around?" Your mind will go through all these things that you could be doing. You could be out cleaning the kitchen. You could be walking the dog. You could be taking the kids somewhere. You're going to go through all these thoughts in your head about what it is that you should go do, something else other than sitting quietly, all by yourself.

Then, during the second 15 minutes, you'll slowly start to unwind. Your breath will become deeper. You'll begin to relax. You may identify some problem that was really bugging you, something you might not have even realized was an issue before. Possible solutions to the problem might come up, but really it is just slowing your mind down.

Then, you will find yourself getting deeper and quieter, but not on purpose. You won't have to force anything. You won't have to try to think about something. You will just be slowly letting it happen. Somewhere between 45 minutes and an hour into it — I don't want you timing yourself, I don't want you to have a watch on, I don't want you to have a clock — but about 45 minutes to an hour into it, an answer will come. It will just pop into your head because you've stayed quiet long enough to listen to yourself or your higher power.

It sounds crazy. I know it sounds off the wall, but I want you to try it.

Evaluate Your Hour

Write a few paragraphs on your experience. Did you like it? Were you uncomfortable? Did anything surprise you about the experience? Did you identify any problems or challenges that you want to address? Did a solution to a problem come to you? Do you feel differently now than you did an hour ago?

Fill the Jar

Here's what happens. We think, "OK. I want to do this. I like what John's talking about. I really enjoyed that hour off the treadmill, but when am I going to fit this in on a regular basis? I can't fit it into my life now the things I already know I want to do much less all this extra stuff."

Imagine that in front of you is an empty Mason jar along with rocks, pebbles and sand. Your task is to fill that jar so everything fits. What would you put in first?

First, imagine filling it like this. Pour the sand in first. Next, put in the pebbles, and finally put in the rocks. You'll have a jar very solidly filled on the bottom with a very unbalanced load on top. Moving that jar around would risk breaking it as the rocks clanked against the glass. It might even be a little top-heavy from the rocks, unstable and easily spilled. You might not have even been able to fit all those rocks inside.

Now, I'd like you to imagine filling it in reverse. Place your big rocks in first, then your pebbles and then your sand. Can you imagine what the jar looks like now? With the big rocks all throughout, the pebbles falling in neatly to the spaces between the rocks, and the sand filling in everywhere else, you'll have a pretty solid jar, evenly filled with much less left over. Imagine tipping that jar over. Not as much would spill out, and all the big rocks would still be inside.

Now, consider the Mason jar as a visualization of an empty day before you. Or an empty year, or 10 years.

What are your big rocks, the things that are most important to you, e.g., kids, family, church, exercise, reading and activities? What's most important to you? You want to put those big rocks in the jar first, and put those things in your calendar first.

What about the pebbles, the things that are important but not nearly as important? Those will go in the jar second. They'll fall into the jar around those big rocks or fill in the empty, usable space on your calendar to help you complete your day and your time.

As for the sand, this is the "stuff" that comes into your life, the things that really are not important but can fill up our days. Leave those things for last. If it doesn't all get into the jar or if it doesn't all get onto your calendar, fine. It's there to keep everything else stable when you need it, but ultimately it's not going to hurt anything if it doesn't all fit.

Unfortunately, what happens for most people is they put sand in there first. All the things that everybody else wants them to do, they do first. All the things that demand their time that really aren't that important, they do first.

Organize Your Rock Collection

This task has two parts. First, I challenge you to really get to know your calendar. If you have a very detailed calendar already, go ahead and use that. You can use the last month or the last six weeks, whatever you think will give you an accurate example of your average habits. If you don't keep a detailed calendar, I recommend spending a week or two keeping a detailed record of your daily activities. Don't change what you're doing as you keep track. Just keep good notes.

Where do you spend the most time? What you find will be a direct reflection of where your priorities currently are. It may not tell you what you love, but it certainly will tell you what you've been valuing, either consciously or unconsciously.

List these items. The more detailed you are, the better you'll be able to understand what you're currently valuing.

Next, divide those items into three groups: Rocks, pebbles and sand.

Then, answer the following questions. Did you find anything surprising? Are any of your rocks missing? Are there any differences between what you currently fill your calendar with and what should be on your calendar? Where might you make changes if you could?

The next step in getting your calendar in line with your priorities is to learn to allocate time. Starting with your rocks, you mark off the time for them on your calendar, devoting enough time to them so they get the attention they need.

I watch and look on a weekly basis and say, "OK, what is most important?" Well, one week for me it might be some family or relationship activities that I'm committed to. I want to allocate time for that. So, if there's a meeting at school, the kids need me for something, if it's date night or horseback riding or whatever the case may be, activities for family and relationships get plugged in first.

The next step for me would be work. I block off time for any appointments I have. Then, I block off time for fitness. By putting these rocks on my calendar, by scheduling them ahead of time, I make the deliberate decision to place the value on them that they deserve.

As you get more efficient at this, you will be able to allocate time for bigger projects. For example, I allocated time to write this book. I had to. If I say, "I'm just going to do it whenever I get time," guess what happens? It never happens. I even allocate time for some social activities and household projects.

This way, you are in control of your time. Your calendar gets filled up with what you want it to accomplish, not what other people have in mind for you. You'll also be more efficient in those times. Some people even take a stopwatch or an egg timer and say, "I'm going to work on this project or this program for the next 15 minutes or 30 minutes." Fit in your time and your passions and allocate time for them. When the timer goes off, you're done doing it. If it's not done, it's not done, but that's the time you've allocated toward that project. You can make adjustments, but you've got to start with blocking out time and go from there.

Prioritize

The other important part of taking control of your calendar is to prioritize your day. Once your day is time-blocked, you have an expectation for what's going to get done that day. Next, decide what the most important activities are that need to get done. Prioritize them as A, B and C or 1, 2 and 3, whichever you prefer. That way you know that you do the As before you go on to the Bs before you go on to the Cs.

It's inevitable that you'll encounter some "fire" that has to be taken care of, someone who needs something from you or some emergency arises. Some of these things are going to happen, and they're going to be uncontrollable.

But, more often than not, you can control it. You can stick to your priorities and say, "This is my time to devote to task XYZ. As soon as I have given it my attention, I can address this fire over here." Sticking to your priorities is going to help you create that balanced life you're looking for. If you don't stick to those priorities, you won't have the time to get done what's important to you, and then who suffers? You do. You won't have the time to do the things you love to do or the time to spend with the people you love or the activities you love because you allowed something else to dictate your priority for the day and to take the place of what should have happened in you day. And if you are giving your time away, you are living someone else's priorities for you.

Either you can choose how you spend your time or someone else will. You can look and say, "I want to time-block, but it sounds so regimented. I don't want to prioritize. I just want to go with the flow. I want to let it evolve. I really want to just be." Sometimes you can do that, but what will inevitably happen is that someone else will choose what's important. Whether it's at work or it's at home, if you don't make the choice, someone else will.

You might say, "Well, John, I have kids at home, and the kids really demand my time."

This is really a great opportunity for you to not only make choices about your priorities for yourself but to model these kinds of values for your kids. If you explain to the kids and say, "You know what, kids, this is Mommy's time. I'm going to take 15 minutes. I want to spend time with you. I want to read your story. I want to hear about your day. I want to help you with your homework. However, this is my 15 minutes. Please don't bother me." They'll respect that. They'll actually love it. They'll also know that this is Mom's time. This could be time that they go do things they want to do.

We can teach our kids to do the same thing, to time-block. We can teach our kids that when we are doing our 15 minutes, they can do their 15 minutes. Ask them how they would like to spend their 15 minutes.

If modeling this kind of behavior for your kids helps motivate you, great. Use that motivation to drive yourself to really stick to your priorities.

Time-blocking might be difficult at first, especially if your schedule isn't consistent and you deal with a lot of unknowns, but I encourage you to give this a go. A lot of different time management options exist.

Use your list to identify your rocks, and then use time blocking to create the seven days ahead.

As you go through the next week, keep notes about how you're feeling about the time-blocking and what challenges you're encountering.

At the end of the week, come back to this journal entry and ask yourself how the week went. Did you feel more in control of your time? Did you encounter any especially difficult challenges? How did you navigate those challenges? What can you do for the upcoming week to make your schedule more your own?

Why Live Your Passion?

Now you've identified what it is you want, your passion, and you've taken ownership of your schedule so your priority obligations are met. Take a moment to congratulate yourself because those are not small tasks. Most people never get there!

But what is the point of having that knowledge and skill? The idea is not just to know yourself or to be a master at meeting your basic needs. We're shooting for something that's at a much higher level here. Your goal in all of this is to find that balance so you truly feel fulfilled. The idea is to incorporate your passion into your life as much as possible.

The more time you spend living your passion, the more you will find you have increased energy and a sense of well-being. You're going to eat better, you're going to sleep better, and you're going to be excited about your day. Even if you look at your calendar and it is full for six straight days, having the ability to say, "You know what? At the end of the week, I get to spend a half-hour doing what I love to do because I've taken these steps to make the changes that will allow me to do it," is going to provide you with more energy and a greater sense of contentment than you'll find anywhere else.

I have seen a lot of folks come in to me for coaching for the first time who are well into the middle of their lives, have established careers and growing families. They'll say something along the lines of how they like their life so far, but they would love to play the piano. They've thought about it for the last 20 years, but they just can't see how it makes sense to start learning to play the piano now.

And I've seen this happen time and again. When folks take their love seriously, they give themselves permission to enjoy their passion and take the steps they need to take to integrate that passion into their lives, they suddenly find their life is easier. They have more energy. They're happier.

I have a client with a 38-foot boat with twin diesel engines. Over the years he spent a lot of money paying mechanics to maintain his boat and engines. He was careful with his money, and got tired of paying others to maintain his boat. So, in his 50s, he went back to school to study diesel mechanics. He found out he was good at working on diesel engines. He became a certified diesel engine mechanic. He loved doing the work. Now he confidently works on his own diesel engines on his boat. And his work makes him happy.

Benefits for You, Your Family and Your Community

I can see some of you coming to me now and saying, "But, John, what does it really matter if I'm happy right now? I've got a mortgage and kids and my retirement to think about. Isn't it awfully selfish to be worried about feeling fulfilled right now?"

My answer to you is a resounding NO. If you are empty and tired, you don't have the strength to help others. If you are rested, full of strength, love and abundance, you have capacity to help others. Once you start making room for your passion your excitement, your energy and your sense of well-being are going to spill over into your family and your community. They're going to see you spending time doing something you love, they're going to see how energized and happy you are, and it's going to affect them. They're going to be energized by it as well.

Also, typically, you're going to find that when you are living your passion, it helps somebody else. Very rarely does your passion only involve you. It's just the way we're all built. Humans are social creatures. Not only is happiness contagious, but it's likely that your passion involves helping other people. Somebody else is going to get a benefit and grow from your unique ability. If your passion is to be the best piano player out there, you're going to find that there are others out there who love your piano playing but can't play them for themselves. You're going to be doing what you do best, and others are going to benefit from the energy and happiness that surrounds your work.

Now it's a matter of taking the steps to do what you love; it's not just thinking about what you love. Take action. Move forward. Become confident. You can do it. Don't just think about it. Go do it. Create a strategy. Take the steps. Do it today.

Please consider how actively pursuing your passion and spending time with your unique ability could help others. Say that you're really passionate about cooking. Well, one of the things that could happen is maybe you should start a part-time catering business. Maybe you could act as a personal chef for someone in need, someone elderly or disabled who could benefit from your help, or maybe you could get involved in the kitchen at your church or your child's school.

Spend some time brainstorming ways that your talent could help other people, whether it's through changing jobs, starting a part-time business, volunteering or involving friends and family. Which of these options appeals to you, or is there another option? What is it about your passion that could benefit others?

Reaching Out to Others

Obviously, since you're this far into the book, you recognize the value of reaching out for advice. The insights and shortcuts that I've discovered over the past 23 years are benefiting others. It was only through pursuing my passion that I developed this book.

Coaching vs. Therapy

Bill Bartlett, a coach I have worked with before, once told me, "John, I do therapy work, but people don't want to go see a therapist. But they will go see a coach." And I thought, "Wow. That makes perfect sense."

We think of a coach as someone we knew when we were kids in high school or college when we were playing sports. We understand a coach as a leader but also as a teacher, a motivator and someone who was looking out for us as we developed our skills.

Now that we're grown up, we likely don't have anyone in our lives we think of as a coach anymore. We're adults, right? We have jobs and kids. Maybe we play rec softball on the weekends. The vast majority of us don't have coaches, but we could definitely all benefit from finding one.

There's no way around the fact that you cannot know everything. You just can't know it all. Too much information exists. I started with a coach for the first time 15 years ago. It was at that moment that my life turned around, and I started to see things a little bit differently. Since then, I've worked with several coaches, each one of whom specialized in areas where I really needed help, such as my understanding of my passion, my approach to communication, my work as an entrepreneur and my ability to develop and cultivate relationships.

My hope is that your life will turn around in the same way.

Keep in mind that your coach could be a pastor or rabbi, he or she could be a personal fitness trainer or a financial consultant. It all depends on where you feel that you need more education or more work to develop your skills. You may not reach out to this person right away. It may take you a while to find the right coach, or you may not have the resources you need right now to work with them. But answering these questions now will prepare you for the day that you do stumble upon the right person or the day that you actively begin searching for them.

Before we move on to the Financial Area, I want to remind you that you'll be back. Whether this is your first time through or your 15th, I promise you that the more you accomplish, the more you will revisit your old work and build upon it. It's when you stop growing, stop changing and stop learning that you stop living your passion.

The Alcoholic

The great German writer Johann Wolfgang von Goethe once said, "The important thing in life is to have a great aim and to possess the aptitude and the perseverance to attain it."

What is the one thing that you can do in the next three days to get you moving on the path to your dreams? If you don't do it in the next three days, you may never do it. There is an alcoholic who knew he needed to quit drinking but never thought it possible. Drinking had become such a huge part of his lifestyle. He worked in a liquor store, his friends liked to drink and he loved being with his friends. However, the drinking had taken such a huge toll on his life, particularly his health, his pancreas was dying. Doctors warned him not to drink. But he continued to drink. After several visits to the hospital, he reached rock bottom. He had made goals of quitting drinking for a year, but he always failed, it was too big of a task. Finally, a friend told him to quit drinking for 20 minutes at a time. At the end of 20 minutes, he said, quit for another 20 minutes, and do this until you get to the end of the day.

Once he had quit for an entire day, he realized it is possible to stay away from alcohol for 24 hours and longer. He stayed sober 20 minutes at a time and, after persistent effort, he had been sober for 30 days, the longest period of sobriety in decades. He felt fantastic. He started running, lifting weights, building up his biceps. He got a new job working in construction. His great aim was to write music, but he had always failed at this effort because he drank too much. Now, writing music came naturally to him. His Facebook posts are inspirational; he is doing so much now. Here is one of his latest posts, "Great day at work and an amazing workout after! Ready for the weekend to get here to kick it with friends in town and maybe do some camping! Life is great! Have a wonderful night all!"

Achieving Financial Balance

Warren Buffett once said, "The chains of habit are too light to be felt until they are too heavy to be broken."

I love this quote because it speaks volumes about our habits becoming so ingrained into our lifestyle, even to our detriment, yet we continue to do them. Bad spending habits create a burden of expense and debt. Good money habits over time can produce amazing results.

This chapter will give you on opportunity to examine your financial picture. In retirement, it is critical to know your bottom-line monthly income requirements. Are you spending more than your income now? What is your budget?

We have to talk about money, because it has a way of touching every other area of our life in a relatively ruthless way.

Money won't make you happy, but lack of money can make you very unhappy.

That's why I spend a lot of my time working with clients as a financial "coach," because my experience as a financial advisor uniquely positions me to help people pursue their dreams by making smart and informed financial choices.

In this section, we will address your beliefs and decisions about money, your current financial picture, your short- and long-term financial goals, and how you can use those goals to create a balanced, fulfilling life.

Here you may feel overwhelmed, underprepared and under qualified to address some of these things, but I promise that we will break these big questions down into small, tangible steps. By understanding your complete financial picture, you will feel more alive, more fulfilled, more balanced, more purposeful and more intentional every single day.

Let me give you an example of where you can go with this. Over their 35 years of marriage together, Andy and Alice earned modest incomes in marketing and social work while pursuing their love of music as a hobby. Using a strategy developed by their advisor, they saved regularly and paid off their house and now have a substantial sum of financial assets and can easily afford to retire. They still work 10 to 20 hours per week while pursuing their passions of visiting art galleries, going to coffee shops, performing music, hosting parties. They often have friends over playing piano, guitar and banjo, singing blue grass songs. They are super creative people, their home is filled with storytelling, hot tea and good food; children and grandchildren visit regularly. Now in their mid-70s, Andy and Alice have overcome some medical issues in recent years, but remain vigorously active. They did retirement right. They are now at their creative height, being around people who share their love of the arts, while traveling to places on their bucket list. They recently returned from a trip to see Abraham Lincoln's home in Springfield, Illinois. Andy and Alice are always smiling. They inspire me. They are the happy ever after; they have a creative and fulfilling retirement.

What Is Most Important About Money to You?

Often I will sit with people and ask them "What is most important about money to you?" Often, folks have never been asked this question or considered the answer, but the answer to this question really strikes to the core of their values and personality.

People answer things like "So I can have security," "So I can have more freedom," "So I can take care of my family," or "So I can give back to my community." "So I can leave a legacy" or "maintain my quality of life."

As we drill down into this complicated question, people find that their core values are playing out in the way that they behave with their money and their attitude toward it.

Now is the time to take a good hard look at what's important to you about money.

Here again we will start by asking the question "What is your 'Why'?"

What is important about money to you? You might also consider this a spiritual question along the lines of "What do you feel called to do with your money?"

You may choose to write about your relationship with money, including childhood experiences that inform how you feel about money now or even recent developments in your life that have impacted your finances.

Ask yourself these questions and listen to yourself carefully. As you write in your journal about these ideas, you may find that you need to take a break or you need to spend two or three journaling sessions addressing the question. You can write a lot right now, or you can write a little and come back to the entry later if you feel you need perspective.

Your "Financial Why" will guide you throughout this area of the book. What do you want money to do for you?

First Things First: What Do You Want?

So, we're focusing on financial affairs and thinking about money. We're thinking about some of the things you may want or you may want to achieve or acquire.

One of the questions that I ask my clients is "What do you really want?" Usually, folks look at me like I'm crazy. They've been on that treadmill, and they haven't asked themselves what they want. They've been busy taking care of their family, church or charity, but what is it that they really want?

Some people say, "I want to make sure I don't run out of money in retirement."

Others want some things that seem out of reach, like a vacation, or to buy some luxuries. When I was growing up, I was always reading the menu from right to left. It wasn't what I really wanted to eat at the local restaurant. It was the cost first, and then I'd see if it was OK that I ordered that item. For some people, that's what they want, to be able to order off a menu without looking at the price.

Some of us just want stuff. We want a boat, a car, some jewelry, a nice house or a second home. For some people, it is retirement. But no matter where we are in our lives, we've got to address this question of the specifics of what we want. We've got to continue that work of getting off the treadmill.

Bucket List

If you've been able to work that off-the-treadmill time into your life on a regular basis at this point, use your next session to address the question: "What do I want?"

If you haven't been able to develop this habit yet, make taking another hour a priority immediately. Go to the quiet space, and get off the treadmill. Take an hour to really think about what you want. Try to do it without time, money or what you're "supposed to do" being a factor. Just really let your imagination go. I know sometimes that's difficult, to put things like this aside, but you're going to benefit from it.

Then, come back to your journal, and write down what you came up with. Right now, create your bucket list. Then, think about this list. Did anything surprise you during your hour off the treadmill? Are there any big-picture items that seem so far away as to be unrealistic? Are there any things that you can see accomplishing in the next three years? Do any of your desires conflict with what others have expected of you?

You Are Here

Let's start at the beginning. Right now, we need to assess where you are, get all of the cards on the table, so-to-speak, so that we can have an accurate and complete picture of your financial life.

Ultimately, we'll want to answer the question "How much do you need?" There is not a one-size-fits-all. It's going to vary from person to person based on what you want and where you are.

I want to stress here that it is important to put in real numbers as you use these tools. Don't use what the media tells you or what your brother-in-law said or what your mechanic told you that you need for retirement. We're going to figure out what you need to hit your financial goals. It's going to be personal, so make it personal.

The first thing, though, is we have got to get a snapshot of your spending habits right now.

Where Do You Spend Money Now?

First and foremost, you need to figure out where you are spending your money, and I mean all of it. It may take you a month to accomplish this, or you may already have the tools at your fingertips. If you are someone who uses your debit card for everything, you can use your bank statements or online banking to quickly identify where your money is going, but many of us use cash or write checks, neither of which gives us the whole picture of our spending. For you, going to Wal-Mart and getting yourself a small notebook that you can put in your pocket may be the best bet. Whatever it is, I want you to document every dollar you spend.

I use QuickBooks for my business, and I use Quicken for my personal stuff. They will show you exactly where all your money goes because you have to put in a category every time you put in some kind of check, payment or transaction. It won't track cash, so if you cash checks and spend money it won't help you there. Use whatever tools you choose, but keep track.

At this point, you might be saying, "John, are you kidding me? You want me to write down every dollar?"

I want to encourage you to do this boring work, because the more detailed you are, the better you are going to be able to plan. Try it for a month, or if you really are impatient, just do it for a week. Start somewhere so you have an idea of where you are right now.

You might choose to pause your work to do this data collection, but I promise that it will be worth it. Come back to this point when you've got your records as complete as they can be.

Your Spending Style

At this point, I want you to take some time to think about the manner in which you spend money day-to-day, not just how much you spend, but the way you act when you spend it and how you think about your transactions.

Do you use cash? If you do, is it kept neatly in your wallet, and do you know how much you have on your person? Do you have a daily or monthly amount that you allocate for spending spontaneously? Do you know how much money is in your bank account on a daily basis, or do you check in weekly, monthly or not at all?

Understanding how you spend money will help you going forward as you work to make changes to what you spend and where you spend it, so we'll be coming back to this later.

Time-Value of Money and the Rule of 72

Before we go further, I want to share an example that may change the way you make purchases. It's called the time-value of money. What the time-value of money means is that every dollar you have, every choice you make, costs something beyond the price tag.

If we choose to save the money, there is a value added to that choice over a certain number of years. If you choose to spend the money, there is a lost opportunity over that same period of time.

For example, let's assume that you are 45 years old, and you want to buy a big screen TV. The TV costs $2,000, and you have the cash to buy it outright.

Let's also assume that if we invested that money somewhere we would have made some kind of interest. Let's say the interest was 7 percent, just for the sake of argument. A common concept in the financial world states that if you select any interest rate and use it to divide the number 72, the result will tell you how often your money will double.

If we're going to get 7 percent on our money, it's going to double every 10 years. If you were 45 years old, planning to retire in 20 years, you could instead take the $2,000 and invest it at 7 percent. By the time you retired, that money would have doubled twice. Our $2,000 would have gone from $2,000 to $4,000, then $4,000 to $8,000.

Instead, you purchased a $2,000 TV. Twenty years later, you probably have a TV that has vastly depreciated in value, and you've also lost out on a $6,000 return on investment.

So, when you are spending money or looking at a purchase or thinking about a $2,000 TV, think about it from the future prospective and the time-value of money because a $2,000 TV doesn't cost $2,000. It actually costs nearly $8,000 because you lost the opportunity to make money on that money as well as retain your original investment. That's what the time-value of money means: Everything has a cost that is more than the price tag.

Now, sit back and ask yourself: Now that you know where your money is going, do you like it or not like it? Are you OK with it, or are you not OK with it? Do any of the numbers surprise you? Did you realize you were spending so much on morning lattes or after-work stops at a convenience store? What do your savings habits look like? What changes would you like to make to your spending habits? Do you see any ways right now to change your habits so there is some extra money to help you achieve your goals?

If you don't like where your money is going, you can change it and seek help. Once you know the real numbers you can choose how to proceed. If you know where your money is going you can say, "Wait a second, I don't want to spend my money there. I want to change it and have it go somewhere else."

If you discovered that you do not like where your money is going, you can make changes. Just like you changed the way you fill your Mason jar in the Personal Area, you can do the same thing with your money.

I want to take a moment here to emphasize: This is not a get-rich-quick scheme. Some people appear to be overnight successes, but dig a little deeper and you will see that a person who fulfills a goal may have worked on that goal a long time. Most of the "overnight" successful people struggled for 10, 15 or 20 years growing, learning, changing habits and saving, and then they became an "overnight" success. It seems "overnight" when someone is working at age 49 but then announces he is retiring early at age

50 to pursue his dream of cycling from Oregon to Argentina. His colleagues react by saying, "Well, how did he do that?"

A Delicate Balancing Act

Now we will tackle your debts. This might not apply to you, but if you are currently struggling with debt, you should complete this section.

Identify the amount of extra money you can free up, whether that's through bringing lunch to work, switching from lattes to coffee, reducing your debt payments to only paying the minimum or whatever works for you. If you have a hard time seeing where the extra money can come from, don't hesitate to contact me. We can discuss other options, like debt consolidation.

Once you know that number, pick one of your debts, whether that's the credit card with the highest interest rate or the smallest balance or a company that hasn't treated you well in the past, and make it the priority. Pay the minimum balance on all of your outstanding debts except for your priority; your priority debt will get all of the extra money you identified in your budget. This method will allow you to pay off one debt quickly, and then apply the money you were using to pay that one bill to the second in your debt priority list and so on. Pretty soon you will be out of debt.

This Is Not Your Grandfather's Retirement

Many years ago, I met a couple that wanted to do more with their money. They had a friend who picked investments for them, but that friend stopped giving advice two years ago and suggested they find a new person. For two years, their money sat in money market accounts not earning anything. These people had worked hard. He was a doctor in a small town; he was busy every day serving his community. She ran the household and worked in real estate. They developed a rental housing business, ran it for 20 years, and made a modest profit each year after expenses. Eventually, she got tired of managing 15 apartments. The upkeep was getting expensive both in terms of time and money. They didn't want to manage all of the painting and carpet replacement. So they sold the business in their mid-60s and decided to retire, knowing their assets may have to last a long time in retirement. They looked for other sources of income. Someone referred them to me. I recommended a financial strategy that would provide steady income with some modest appreciation. After many years of living in retirement, the doctor died in his 90s. She continues to live today from an income portfolio. The message here is they found a way to live a long time in retirement without running out of money. You can, too. Studies show that healthy retirees tend to live a long time in retirement. You will have to be prepared.

Retirement. Now, that's a pretty loaded concept. For some people, it's that glorious time when they move to Florida and golf all day and sit side-by-side with their love in Adirondack chairs in the evening waiting for the cabana boy to come by with their cocktails. But does everybody think that? Well, I hate to bust your bubble with retirement reality, but it's not like that anymore. Or maybe your reaction is "Oh, thank goodness, John, that is not what I want whatsoever."

The truth be told, if you're in your 50s, that was your parents' retirement. This is not the way you retire. It's not going to look like that. It's going to be totally different.

Today, I am seeing that most people want to do more. They want to go do something, to give back, to make a contribution. Most people still have a lot of things that they want to do. Retirement is not going to be your family putting you out to pasture. It's going to be the next phase in your life. You're going to move on to something bigger and something better. You're also going to care less what other people think. Then, that's when the real you comes out. That's the good news.

Unfortunately, a little sticky part is you have to have money to be able to make those choices and have good options. Retirement is not about the person who acquires the most. It's about giving yourself what you want and pursuing your passion.

Let me ask you this: If time or money were not a factor, what would you do?

Think about it for a second. Now, before you get too far, I'm going to stop you to ask: Is that a fair question?

For most of us, time and money are factors. We don't live off trust funds or have piles of money hidden in the basement to just go do what we want. We don't have unlimited time. So, time and money are factors. The reality is we have to live within our means.

However, there is also another reality, one in which you may have enough to do what you want, you just don't know it.

Now, I want you to spend some time answering that first question. Keep in mind that, until you truly imagine the retirement you want, you won't know if you can have it.

When you think about retirement, what does it mean to you? Where would you live? What would you spend your days doing? Be detailed.

Retirement may not cost what you think. It could be far less. Start dreaming, and then we'll start planning.

Be Prepared

How much money is enough?

This task is going to use all the work that you've accomplished so far in your Financial Area, to help you get together a plan for how to save for your future. Even if you're not ready right now, this section will be of use to you because it will help prepare you for the day you are ready. It will help you to envision a future where you are saving for retirement.

A U.S. Government Accountability Office analysis found half of households age 55 and older have no retirement savings (such as in a 401(k) plan or an IRA). According to GAO's analysis of the 2013 Survey of Consumer Finances, many older households without retirement savings have almost no other resources, such as a defined-benefit plan or nonretirement savings, to draw on in retirement. For example, among households age 55 and older, about 29 percent have neither retirement savings nor a pension. Households that have retirement savings generally have other resources to draw on, such as nonretirement savings and pension plans. Among those with some retirement savings, the median amount of those savings is about $104,000 for households age 55 to 64 and $148,000 for households age 65 to 74. Social Security provides most of the income for about half of households age 65 and older.[2]

The Retirement Analysis

This analysis is going to piggyback on the income analysis. The Retirement Analyzer is a tool that will help you determine how much income you need to live the life you want to live. You can call me to set up a time to go through the Retirement Analyzer, or you can use some free tools online. The free tools aren't going to be as comprehensive as what I can help you do, and they're not going to be personalized. If, after using the online calculators, you have still got questions, drop me a line, and we can take a look at your situation.

The way that you are going to live the life you want to live is two-fold. You need time. You need money. The Retirement Analyzer will help you examine whether or not you are on the right

---

[2] Government Accountability Office. GAO-15-419. May 12, 2015. "Most Households Approaching Retirement Have Low Savings." http://www.gao.gov/products /GAO-15-419. Accessed Oct. 27, 2016.

track and identify places you can make changes if necessary. That should create more time and alleviate a heck of a lot of stress.

Take a moment right now to come up with a ballpark number of what you want to have saved by the time you retire. Take into account how much money you need each month to do the kinds of things you want to do in your retirement.

First Things First: Pay Less to the IRS

"The tax collector must love poor people, he's creating so many of them," wrote William Vaughn, former columnist with The Kansas City Star.

Vaughn is a jokester, but there is a little truth in what he says. Without proper guidance, people often pay taxes unnecessarily to the government. The tax code is very complex. Let us pay no more than we have to. There are multiple ways to reduce your tax burden. I will list a few ideas here that may help you retain a little more of your income.

One Option: Starting a Business

Starting a business may be an option for you depending on your lifestyle and your long-term goals. Business is the one place that still allows you to take some deductions that can be carried over. For example, if you work out of your home, you could use some of these deductions: The phone you use if you make any kind of calls for business or your cars — or at least their mileage. A myriad of possibilities exist when it comes to business expenses that are not as easy to claim as an individual. However, make sure you develop a business plan before you go into business for yourself. One of the easiest ways to lose money is to start a business without a plan. Your business plan should show exactly how much revenue you need each month to pay for expenses. You should also do a market survey to make sure there are customers out there demanding the services/products of your business.

Commonly Missed Personal Deductions

Moving Expenses for Your First Job: You can deduct your moving expenses for job relocation purposes. If you have moved over 50 miles, you can deduct 20 cents per mile, parking fees and tolls, and you can also deduct your car expenses and the cost of moving yourself and your belongings to your new home.

Student Loans Interest Paid: Student loan interest paid is a biggie. The IRS does require that you pay the student loan to qualify for the deduction. If your parents pay back your student loan, the IRS uses this as your parents giving you the money so you can pay your debt. However, if you're not being claimed as a dependent, you can qualify to deduct up to $2,500 of your student loan interest paid by your parents.

College Tuition: If your income is too high to qualify for the whole credit of the lifetime learning credit but you pay college tuition for yourself, your spouse or a dependent, you can still deduct up to $4,000 on your tax return.

Out-of-Pocket Charitable Contribution: It's pretty much common knowledge that you can deduct charitable contributions on your personal taxes, but when you are donating to a charity and you make more than $150,000, there is a phase out on your personal return. However, if you make that contribution from your corporation or from your business, there isn't a phase out. So make your contribution from your company. This is a greater win for everybody. If you don't have to pay tax on the contribution, then how much more would you give?

Charitable Remainder Trust: Say, for example, that you bought a stock for $10,000 and now it's worth $100,000. Well, if we sell it, what happens? You've got to pay capital gains tax on the difference between the $10,000 and the $100,000. However, if you donate it, you can get the tax deduction, and you can carry that forward for a number of years. If I give $100,000 and I make $30,000 a year, I can only deduct 50 percent of the gift, or $50,000, but I can carry it forward for a couple of years. Meanwhile, I gave that asset to my favorite charity. When that charity sells it, they get the whole $100,000, and you've saved a ton in taxes.

Are you someone who has one W-2 and just takes your taxes into H&R Block every year, collects a small refund and moves on, or is filing taxes every year akin to pulling the teeth of an angry lion?

Either way, take time on this journal to brainstorm some ways you can keep more of your income for yourself through tax deductions. Take a moment to do an internet search for commonly missed deductions, and see if any apply to you. Making this list now will enable you to stay organized, keep receipts and be prepared for April 15.

Often we see people using tax preparers, not tax planners. Seek wisdom from tax planners. This way you can work on minimizing your tax burden over several years, using sound and helpful advice from a quality tax professional.

So, now you know where you are and what you want. You know what your real numbers are. You have a good idea of some of the steps that you can take to improve your financial picture. I hope you're feeling a little bit more confident. For this task, we're going to look ahead at ways you can stay on track and keep up the momentum you've gained by doing the hard work you've started.

PERSONAL WEALTH STRATEGY

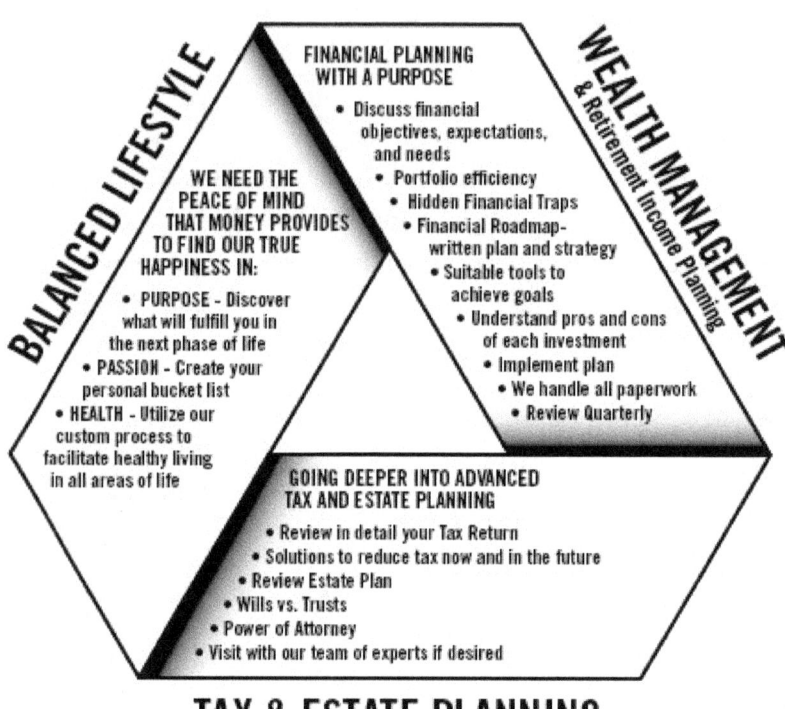

BALANCED LIFESTYLE

WEALTH MANAGEMENT
& Retirement Income Planning

FINANCIAL PLANNING WITH A PURPOSE
- Discuss financial objectives, expectations, and needs
- Portfolio efficiency
- Hidden Financial Traps
- Financial Roadmap- written plan and strategy
- Suitable tools to achieve goals
- Understand pros and cons of each investment
- Implement plan
- We handle all paperwork
- Review Quarterly

WE NEED THE PEACE OF MIND THAT MONEY PROVIDES TO FIND OUR TRUE HAPPINESS IN:
- PURPOSE - Discover what will fulfill you in the next phase of life
- PASSION - Create your personal bucket list
- HEALTH - Utilize our custom process to facilitate healthy living in all areas of life

GOING DEEPER INTO ADVANCED TAX AND ESTATE PLANNING
- Review in detail your Tax Return
- Solutions to reduce tax now and in the future
- Review Estate Plan
- Wills vs. Trusts
- Power of Attorney
- Visit with our team of experts if desired

TAX & ESTATE PLANNING

Be Honest

No single retirement portfolio looks the same as someone else's. You're not a number. You're a unique individual with values, plans and goals. If you want something different than what everybody else has, you have to do something different. About 50 percent of Americans retire on Social Security alone. As a saver, you have made different choices. You are way ahead of the crowd. You're going against the grain. Most people don't save, most people don't get it or they want somebody else to take care of them. You're different, so embrace your differences. Be proud of what you've done.

Seek Accountability

Don't be afraid to ask for help, and be honest about who you are and what you want and need. Look for experts who can help you. Look for groups in the community where you can share your experience and learn from others. Consider hiring a financial advisor who can help you develop a strategy and offer guidance and support.

Set Concrete Goals

It is so important that it bears repeating: Your path to success is extremely dependent upon clearly articulating goals. Once you've identified places you can make changes and ways that you can implement those changes, write those goals down, and put them in a prominent place, such as on a bulletin board by the front door, on your refrigerator or on your computer's desktop. This will help you to stay consistently focused on your goals and remind you what you're working for.

A Diversified Portfolio

There are multiple ways to invest your money, but the most important factor is diversification. Don't put your eggs in one basket. Don't risk everything on one venture. I know one investor who has nearly all his assets in one stock. What if that stock were to go bankrupt? He would lose his retirement. This happened with employees of Enron. Many employees had the majority of their retirement savings in Enron stock. When the company bankrupted, they lost everything. In my opinion, it's wiser to own a diverse portfolio of stocks, bonds, cash, insurance, real estate and annuities that guarantee income for life, plus death benefits.

The Fiduciary Standard

The fiduciary standard of care requires that a financial advisor act solely in the client's best interest when offering personalized financial advice. Unfortunately, not all financial professionals are held to this standard. Many are held to the suitability standard instead, which requires professionals to make recommendations that are suitable for their clients, but doesn't always mean a product has to be "best" for a client.

I believe the fiduciary standard is a good thing for clients because it is a higher standard of care. I have been adhering to this standard in my practice for 15 years because I believe it is the right thing to do.

Four Buckets

Here is my Four Bucket approach toward retirement. I use this in my work to help people like you design retirement strategies with the aim of keeping you on the path toward financial confidence and independence.

People approaching retirement or those in retirement have worked very hard to build up their wealth. They don't want to lose it. They don't want to outlive their wealth. With the rising cost of health care, it can be very expensive to live in retirement, even if you have cut out other expenses. Retirees want enough income to pay their bills and enjoy retirement. And if you are healthy going into your retirement years, you may live a long time in retirement. Medical advances have improved survival rates for life-threatening diseases. People with chronic ailments are able to lead more active lives with the help of modern medicine. Can you afford to live 20 years or even 30 years in retirement? It's not uncommon for a person to retire at age 66 and still be retired 30 years later. I have at least 10 clients who have been retired for about 20 years or more. One couple retired when they were 61 and 62; they have been retired for 25 years. Now they are in their late 80s and still going strong. With a dependable and well-defined financial strategy, they have been able to do what they want to do. The husband went into art and has become a wonderful artist.

Risk Management Strategies - Asset Allocation

| Cash | Income | Short-Term Growth | Long-Term Growth |

Bucket No. 1 will be the Cash Bucket. This bucket has enough money to pay for incidentals and emergency situations; it has three to six months' living expenses. The money must be liquid and accessible. Bank checking, savings and money market accounts would serve this purpose.

Bucket No. 2. This is the Income Bucket. How much income do you need monthly? The age you decide to accept Social Security will affect your decision here. These income bucket assets could include a fixed index annuity, dividend-paying stocks, bonds or real estate investment trusts. There are pros and cons with each one of these assets. Each asset carries some level of risk. Dividend-paying stocks carry risk of loss of principal if the stock market goes down, but deliver quarterly income. Bonds and bond funds face risks of loss of value from rising interest rates. An annuity can provide regular steady income, but interest earnings are limited and penalties are imposed if money is withdrawn early. You want to make sure you are in the right assets that fit your risk tolerance, your comfort level and your time horizon.

Bucket No. 3. This is the Short-Term Bucket, with investments that have a time horizon of three to five years away. Perhaps the money here is for several goals, including a trip to Africa or a cruise through the Mediterranean. A good institutional money manager can provide stocks, bonds or ETFs that could help you work toward your desired outcome.

Bucket No. 4. This is the Long-Term Bucket, with target use in five to 10 years. For this bucket, you might consider a growth approach, meaning investments here will appreciate over time but likely will experience peaks and valleys because financial markets fluctuate and carry varying levels of risk and volatility. But there are ways to mitigate risks. Diversifying investments is one way to reduce risks. You may want to consider a blend of small capital stocks, mid-cap and large-cap stocks, along with perhaps international stocks, growth stocks and value stocks. You will probably want to rebalance these investments every year. I like institutional money managers to fill this role.

Hypothetical example — A couple with $1 million might consider:

$50,000 for the cash bucket.

$400,000 for the income bucket

$150,000 for the short-term bucket

$400,000 for the long-term bucket.

Everyone's situation is unique and the choice of allocations will ultimately depend on each individual's risk tolerance and financial objectives. However, the four-bucket approach can put you in control of your wealth while ignoring the noise of the daily business news. You won't have to worry if Greece is going to default on its loans. You can live your life freely to do what you want. The four-bucket approach is designed to give you the confidence you deserve, knowing you have the cash and income to ride out the financial storms.

Low Volatility Investing

Clients who are risk averse may want to consider creating a portfolio of investments with lower volatility than the general market. By using a stock's "beta," a measure of volatility, it's possible to create a portfolio with low volatility.

One study by Research Associate's Feifei Li and Philip Lawton shows that low-risk stocks have historically outperformed high-risk stocks.[3]

A beta of 1 means a stock moves with the general stock market. A stock with a beta of 1.5 means the stock is going to react up or down 1.5 times the market, or with 50 percent higher volatility on the upside or downside. So, on a day when the S&P 500 is up 1

---

[3] Feifei Li, Philip Lawton. Research Affiliates. September 2014. "True Grit: The Durable Low Volatility Effect." Fundamentals. https://www.researchaffiliates.com /documents/True%20Grit_The%20Durable%20Low%20Volatility%20Effect%20pdf.pdf. Accessed Oct. 27, 2016.

percent, your stock may go up 1.5 percent — a higher return than the general market. But on the downside, this is also true; you will lose more than the general market.

It is foolish to assume that taking on more risk will produce higher returns. We all want the sure thing in business with no risk, but this is nearly impossible to find. But it is possible to find low-beta stocks with steadily rising dividends.

If you are looking to achieve a 5 to 7 percent return, you might want to consider this approach: If you can get 3 percent of that return from dividends and interest, then you only need 2 or 3 percent appreciation. This means you don't have to take on too much risk to reach your goal. High quality consumer stocks and utilities carry a low beta or low volatility relative to the general market. And they pay dividends.

Feifei Li and Philip Lawton said research shows investors like high-risk stocks, they are enamored of the story of investing in a startup and getting rich. Many investors are not interested in modest income and growth. They are out there looking for the next Apple. Li and Lawton argue these low-beta stocks actually trade at a discount to the broad market. With this knowledge, a good institutional investor can pick up these assets and provide steady dividend income to his clients.

One myth some advisors subscribe to is the 4 Percent Rule. Let's say, hypothetically, you have $1 million. This rule of thumb says you take 4 percent out each year and your investments should earn enough gains to recover your withdrawals. The hope is that you won't lose your principal. But a good strategy is not based on hope alone. What if your investment drops 20 percent? Now you have $800,000. Now, 4 percent of that is $32,000, substantially less than your previous $40,000 annual draw. Bull stock markets don't run forever, so there will always be corrections, but are you prepared for one? What kind of portfolio should you have? Perhaps a wiser strategy is to create a well-diversified portfolio that does not rely solely on the market for income.

Watch out for fees. There are multiple fund companies who charge over 3 percent. Some funds have sales charges that can be up to 5 percent. Trading costs are usually passed onto the mutual fund customer. Imagine investing $100,000 and the manager whacks off 3 percent in fees; that is $3,000 leaving your account. You can lower your fees. Studies show lower fees actually lead to higher returns. It makes sense.

Forbes said the average expense ratio for a mutual fund is 0.90 percent. These are fees that you can see on their financial reports. But there are other costs, including trading costs. We often see new clients with portfolios with a total of 3 percent in fees, trading costs and expenses.[4]

"Theoretically, one might think active management leads to higher returns. That is not the case. A growing body of evidence shows that higher expense funds do not, on average, perform better than lower expense funds," reported Simon Moore in a Forbes article dated Sept. 29, 2014.[5]

I believe a good advisor can help you find funds that have a solid history of performance without a high fee structure. Find an advisor who has access to the entire universe of funds and has your best interests in mind. Someone who can help you craft a strategy that matches your goals. It is often possible to drop fees by 1 percent of assets under management. On $500,000, that is a lot of money, amounting to $5,000 per year in savings.

---

[4] Ty A. Bernicke. Forbes. April 4, 2011. "The Real Cost of Owning a Mutual Fund." http://www.forbes.com/2011/04/04/real-cost-mutual-fund-taxes-fees-retirement-bernicke.html. Accessed Oct. 27, 2016.

[5] Simon Moore. Forbes. Sept. 29, 2014. "Get More By Paying Less for Your Funds." http://www.forbes.com/sites/simonmoore/2014/09/29/get-more-by-paying-less-for-your-funds/#5d5c092e6320. Accessed Oct. 27, 2016.

Let's take a look at what one of my clients' portfolios might look like when they come in for a meeting. This couple had worked hard and saved in multiple accounts of mutual funds. Sally and Bob had about $1 million worth of investments. When a client is considering coming to our firm, we conduct an initial meeting to get to know one another. If they like what they see, we then conduct an Investment Organizer, which is deep-dive look into their current financial situation. We produce a detailed document for a small fee. We look at all their financial assets and liabilities. We also ask them about their monthly income needs. As part of the analysis, we take a hard look at what they are invested in currently, their returns and fees. Sally and Bob were paying an average of 1.03 percent in fees in their mutual funds. On top of that, they were paying 1.5 percent of the portfolio in a fee to a financial advisor. So their total fees each year were 2.53 percent. On $1 million, that is $25,300 per year in fees. We saw that using some different products could lower their fees and reduce their risk, ultimately saving them $11,000 in annual fees. That is about $916.66 per month. That money could be used toward their monthly income needs.

One fund family that we utilize is Dimensional Fund Advisors. One of the reasons I like this fund family is their low fees and steady long-term performance. DFA funds are not about trying to hit home runs. Some hedge fund managers will bet the farm on one investment that they hope is a winner. DFA does not work that way. Rather than looking for home-run hitters, DFA is looking for steady hits to get on base and keep the players moving around the bases.

You might think of it like this: The Kansas City Royals won the World Series in 2015. Some of the team's players almost never hit a home run. A good example is Jarrod Dyson. I've seen him get on base with infield hits because he is so fast. One of the extraordinary moments during that World Series was when Jarrod Dyson achieved a rare feat: An in-the-park home run. The ball was not caught in center field and bounced away from the outfielder. Dyson was already approaching third and ran to home plate before the outfielder could throw the ball home. Another great team member that year was Eric Hosmer. This guy gets on base a lot. He drives his teammates home. Steady, reliable hitters win games. DFA funds invest in steady reliable investments that produce reasonable returns. That's all we need.

Three-Day Rule

Consider answering the question: What is the one thing that you can do in the next three days to get you taking action toward realizing your goals?

If you don't do it in the next three days, you won't do it. Pick one goal from this area that you can implement in the next three days to help move you toward your personal dreams.

The Process

Marcus Lemonis, host of CNBC's "The Profit," often talks about people, process and product. If a business has the right combination of all three, it can be successful. When he talks about the process, he often talks about streamlining the process to make it more efficient. In the financial services industry, you need a skilled financial advisor with a good process and decent products.

At John Navin & Associates Inc., we have an excellent staff with a proven process and access to excellent financial products with reasonable or low fees. Our process is customer friendly. We adhere to the fiduciary standard, meaning we do what's in the best interest of our clients. We do not hard sell any product, because our fee is the same, regardless of the product. Our process can be broken down into three meetings. The first is a get-to-know-you meeting. This gives you and us a chance to meet one another.

JNA FINANCIAL PROCESS

DISCOVERING FINANCIAL OBJECTIVES

To begin the process, we will explore the life you want to create. We will examine your current financial situation and then use this as the foundation to help you develop a clearer picture of your future.

- ► Review your financial profile,
- ► Open dialogue on goals, objectives and expectations
- ► Organize and evaluate account statements
- ► Review John Navin & Associates' planning process
- ► Decide on next steps

LIFESTYLE MAXIMIZER

Before your next meeting, John Navin & Associates will take a more in-depth look at your accounts and market values. We will process Morningstar reports, an investment organizer and your retirement analysis.

- ► Review retirement analyzer
- ► Review Social Security analyzer
- ► Portfolio efficiency
- ► Hidden financial traps
- ► Tax planning overview
- ► Discuss account options

FINANCIAL ROADMAP

- ► Written financial plan and strategy
- ► Identify tools to help you work towards your personal goals
- ► Understand the pros and cons that go with these choices
- ► Assess risk involved with each choice and investment
- ► Address any desired changes, discuss options and modify plan to meet needs
- ► Become comfortable and familiar with tools utilized

IMPLEMENTATION

Throughout the process, you can be assured that we will handle the following with dedication and thoroughness:

- ► Fulfillment
- ► Transferring of all accounts
- ► Updating investment organizer with changes made
- ► Delivery of any documents for your files
- ► 1st quarterly review
- ► Estate planning overview
- ► Balanced lifestyle discussion

DESTINATION KNOWN

At John Navin & Associates, we value arming our clients with the most up-to-date information and empowering them to make educated decisions in the matters that directly impact their financial, personal and physical lives. We do this by cultivating strong relationships and a sense of community for our clients through communication and education.

Our clients benefit from our concierge services:

- ► Monthly or quarterly calls
- ► Newsletters
- ► Workshops and seminars
- ► Quarterly reviews with account snapshot summaries
- ► VIP event invitations

In this first meeting, you might talk about your financial objectives, your expectations and needs. If someone likes what they see and we believe we are a good fit for each other, we go to the next step. In the second step, we take a hard look at your financial situation, your current assets and liabilities, your goals and objectives, and how much monthly income you might need in retirement. Using your information, we put together what's called a "Lifestyle Maximizer" or "Portfolio Stress Test."

This document will show you exactly what you are currently paying in fees for your investments, their performance and their risk. We develop a proposed portfolio with suitable tools to achieve your goals.

We provide the pros and cons of each investment. If you like what you see, we meet a third time to begin implementation of the financial strategy.

What I often find is that clients have no idea whether they can afford to retire.

"You mean there is a way for me to retire?" they often say in a state of disbelief. But when I show them in black and white how to maximize their lifestyle in retirement, their dream of retiring suddenly looks like a real possibility.

We don't judge a book by its cover, because you never know how much money a person has just by looking at him. I've seen cases where a farmer likes to wear coveralls and drive an old pickup truck. His boots are scuffed up and his shirt has a tear in it. But when the farmer shows his financial paperwork, it turns out he is worth $4 million. And I have seen just the opposite. A couple is dressed perfectly with the latest fashionable clothes. They drive an expensive car. They vacation in the Bahamas. But when we look at their finances, we discover they are in shambles. They have tons of credit card debt, mortgages, student loans and second mortgages. And their net worth is near zero. The point here is this: We treat everyone with respect. We work with clients as a team. I often say, "You have trusted us with your hard-earned savings, a trust we don't take lightly."

Achieving Physical Balance

Before Jack Stevens retired, he told his friends he was going to laugh at them when he saw them hustling to make a buck while he was doing nothing in retirement. Jack had worked many years and saved diligently for retirement. When Jack finally retired, he sat on the couch and watched TV. His legs went to sleep. Circulation stopped. His legs were cold. He could barely walk. He saw a doctor, who checked him over. His blood pressure was a little high, but not high enough to require medication. His heart and lungs were OK. So why did his legs fall asleep? The doctor asked him what his occupation was before retirement, and Jack said he was a mechanic who worked on farm machinery and trucks all day. He rarely ever sat down. He was always on his feet. The doctor told him to get off the couch and get some exercise every day. "If you don't use your legs, you are going to lose them," the doctor said.

Jack is a real person (although his name is changed here). Yet Jack is also a metaphor for what's wrong in America. Too many people are on the couch doing nothing but playing video games, watching TV or binge-watching "Game of Thrones." No one wants to exercise. Combined with indulgent eating habits, Americans are in terrible shape. About 68 percent of Americans are overweight and about 35 percent are obese. That is a staggering statistic. There are so many mixed messages about this reality. But if you are serious about improving your health, there is a way to lose weight and get healthy. I know. I have been there. For several years, I was very much a part of the 68 percent of Americans who were overweight, but I am not now.[6]

You may have some preconceived notions about your physical health, wellness, dieting and self-care. So many conflicting, harsh and even incorrect messages are out there on TV, on the internet and even coming from friends and family, and many of us feel like giving up and just eating a dozen doughnuts while we watch late-night TV.

In this area, you are going to work to let go of those attitudes. You will address your feelings about food, exercise, wellness and health. You will identify your short- and long-term physical goals. You will discover how you can re-think your health to create a balanced, fulfilling life by breaking things down into small, tangible steps. By understanding your complete physical picture, you will feel more alive, more fulfilled, more balanced, more purposeful and more intentional every day.

A Bit of Background

In my youth, I was an athlete. I enjoyed baseball, football, golf and wrestling. I wrestled and played rugby in college. I graduated college with a degree in physical education. Physical activity was important to me, and my lifestyle was built around it. However, when I got out of school, started working and had kids, I didn't continue all the parts of that lifestyle.

I wasn't wrestling, but I ate like a wrestler out of season. Wrestlers have a tendency to eat like crazy in the offseason, and then they starve and cut weight tremendously when they're in season.

---

[6] National Institute of Diabetes and Digestive and Kidney Disease. 2012. "Overweight and Obesity Statistics." https://www.niddk.nih.gov/health-information/health-statistics/Pages/overweight-obesity-statistics.aspx. Accessed Oct. 27, 2016.

Well, my entire life had become offseason. Before I knew it, I was pushing 260 pounds, and I thought, "This is crazy. I'm 5' 8". I don't need to be 260 pounds." I had doctors telling me that I had a weight problem. Now, my argument here was "I don't have a weight problem, I have a height problem. If I was 6' 10", I'd be perfectly in the right weight."

But the truth of the matter was, I am 5' 8" and, yes, I had a weight problem.

So, I said it was time to do something, time to make a change. Physical balance has always been a personal passion of mine, and now I live it. I weigh 190 (and still losing) and participate in triathlon events, and I'm proud to say I am an Ironman.

I do want to say that I am not a doctor or a medical professional, so before you begin to make changes, I encourage you to discuss it with your health care professional.

My hope for you is not that you'll suddenly start making physical balance your passion or your calling, but that you will use this area of the plan to drop a few pounds, build physical confidence, feel better in your own body and ultimately have more energy and strength to pursue your passions.

What Is Your Physical Why?

We will start the Physical Area just like we did the other two areas and ask the question "What is your Why?"

By this, I mean, what is important to you about effecting physical changes in your life, and why do you want these changes? What is important about health to you? You might also consider this a spiritual question along the lines of "How can your physical health affect your ability to pursue your true calling?"

You may choose to write about your relationship with food or exercise, including childhood experiences that inform how you feel about your body or your health now or even recent developments in your life that have impacted your physical health.

Ask yourself these questions, and listen to yourself carefully. As you write in your journal about these ideas, you may find that you need to take a break or that you need to spend two or three journaling sessions addressing the question. You can write a lot right now, or you can write a little and come back to the entry later if you feel you need perspective.

Your "Physical Why" will guide you throughout this area of the plan.

Oh the Humanity

I really want to emphasize here that we are all human. We're all subject to stress, financial pressures, family worries, health problems, everything. You are human, and you have a body. That body, just like your finances, needs your attention, your goal-setting and your hard work to remain vibrant and support you as you pursue your passions.

Generally as we age, we lose a pound of muscle every year. This process happens naturally because that's the way we were built as humans. But our bodies try to maintain balance whether we're helping it or not, so what often happens is that the pound of muscle gets replaced by a pound of fat. Your body, left to its own devices while you worry about paying the mortgage and getting the kids to bed, does the best it can, but ultimately the result is that you lose energy, strength, stamina and — perhaps what bothers us the most — your youthful appearance.

This is happening to everybody. So, I want you to give yourself a break. Give yourself permission to be human inside your human body. Just like you're not likely to wake up tomorrow and win the lottery, you're even less likely to wake up and suddenly have all the strength, stamina and health you desire. Just like the Personal and Financial areas, this is a process.

At some point in your life, you've probably said, "You know what, I want to get fit. I want to eat better. I want to do something different." But you don't get much farther than that. Why? Because saying that is just like daydreaming. To break that cycle, you need goals. You need to set out specific steps you can take to reach those goals. The Physical Area is going to help you set goals and give you a step-by-step guide to achieve those goals.

Another important thing to keep in mind is something I said in the introduction and that is to be a friend to yourself. You won't get anywhere judging yourself for where you are now, what you look like or how many stairs you can climb before you get winded. Perhaps more than any other area, the Physical Area requires that you be kind to yourself. This will keep you motivated and committed to pursuing your goals.

Get to Know Your Body

First and foremost, you need to figure out where you are right now when it comes to your body and how you use it. It may take some time to accomplish this, or you may already have all the information you need. If you are not as organized, you may want to go get another little notebook that you can put in your pocket to document your physical activities, eating habits and health issues. Some great websites and smartphone apps are out there that can help you.

However you gather this information, you need to collect the following: What you eat over the course of a week; how much and what type of physical activity you do; how much sleep you get and the quality of that sleep; your height, weight and pertinent measurements (like blood pressure, cholesterol and blood sugar); what medicines, vitamins and supplements you take on a chronic and acute basis; how much and how often you smoke or drink; health history highlights, including current health conditions and previous surgeries or hospitalizations; contact information for your health care providers; and contact information and benefits coverage information from your health insurer, including a copy of your insurance card.

I also recommend going to your doctor for a physical at this time just to get as clear a picture as possible. You might also discuss your experience with him or her to make sure that any changes you plan to make are right for you and your unique situation.

At this point, you might be saying, "John, are you kidding me? You want me to write down every little thing?"

Again, just start with one small step. Write as much as you can. I want to encourage you to do this boring work because the more detailed you are, the better you are going to be able to know yourself and set goals. So, try it for a month or, if you really are impatient, just do it for a week.

Weigh-In

This topic is tough for some people, just as the point where you got a clear picture of where and how you spend your money. I want to encourage you to not be scared of writing down real numbers and honest thoughts here, or in any of your journals, for that matter.

Now that you've collected a clear picture of your health as it stands, how do you feel about this? Are there any places where you wish you could make a change? Do you want to lose weight? Do you want to be able to run a mile? Do you want to move more during your day? Do you want to seek to lessen your dependence on medications? Do you want to eat more healthfully? Do you want to get more sleep?

Then, consider your weaknesses. Do you simply love the tradition of pizza on Friday nights with your family more than just the pizza you're eating? Does your morning latte really make you happy in addition to the caffeine rush? Do Sunday mornings lying in bed reading the paper help you to de-stress and motivate you for the week ahead? Why are these indulgences important to you, and are there any of them you aren't willing to give up?

Keeping in mind your Physical Why, what specific changes could you make in your day that would also motivate you and improve your quality of life?

How Long Do You Want to Live?

If you could pick your age to pass away, when would it be? Now, this sounds like a funny question because you usually don't get asked that, and most people say, "John, I can't control when I'm going to pass away." Well, I'm going to beg to differ. I'm going to tell you that I'm not trying to play God or be something that I'm not, but what I am going to state is that what you think about comes true, whether that's good or bad. Whatever you think about comes true.

So, if you had your health and you were in great shape, how old would you be? Pick a number. You might think, "I don't want to live past 80. I don't want to be old. I don't want someone to take care of me. I don't want to be a burden on society. I really don't want to be one of those old people in a nursing home, shuffling my feet down the hallway, sitting in a chair in a corner." Well, I don't want that for you either. That's not what I'm picturing for you, and that's not what I'm picturing for me. I was asked how old I want to live. My answer was 115. With time, health, money, energy and passion, why not 115?

How Much Time Do You Need?

Take the time right now to picture it for yourself. If you had your health, money, choices, the ability to do what you love, how old would you be? What would your number be? How much time do you need to accomplish the goals you set out in the Personal and Financial areas?

If you have some very specific things you want to do or see in your life before you die, write them down here and then think about how much time you need to actually do that. By this, I mean something like, "I need one week to drive out to Branson, Missouri, and see Willie Nelson, and I'll need to work for 80 hours to save the money to pay for the trip."

It's very easy to come to the Physical Area and end up feeling discouraged. You may not see how you have the time, money or energy to make physical changes and accomplish all that you want.

However, I want to reiterate that the very act of understanding where you are and envisioning where you want to be is a very powerful tool when it comes to making changes in your life.

Department of Energy

Setting aside time, money and physical limitations, we all have activities in our life that we enjoy, and those activities require energy. When it comes to your energy, if you had a little bit more, what would you do with it? Would you garden? Would you kick around a soccer ball with your kids? Would you repaint the living room? Would you curl up with a good book while sitting in the sun?

We all have a finite amount of time, and each day we must choose how to use our time, whether we use it on things we enjoy or on things we do because we have to, such as making dinner, shopping, putting in a full day at work or doing the laundry. You're spending your time budget on those just as much as you are on gardening or soccer.

We can't add more hours to the day, but we can increase the amount of energy we have. What if you had more energy?

Just like we all have many ways of making a living, whether we're coffee baristas or biomedical engineers, we all have the capability to increase our energy reserves in different ways, and we can also spend them in different ways.

Bottom line, just like we need money, we need energy, and we've got to figure out how to both generate it and use it in ways that are satisfying, ways that fulfill us.

Just One More Thing in Your Day

Have you noticed you're giving up things you enjoy because at the end of the day you're just too tired or can't focus? If you had some extra energy, even just a little, what is one activity that you would add into your day?

Energy Source

Let's start with nutrition. I don't just mean calories in, calories out. A lot of people think that way. While it can help to be mindful of the calories you consume, what I want you to start with is the quality of those calories. Most people think, thanks to social conditioning and often a lack of education on the subject, "I have to diet. I have to cut back. I can't eat this much." which is directly followed by the thought, "But I'm starving all the time. I'm craving Krispy Kreme."

When we think about scarcity and cutting back, it sends us into this mode where we become anxious and filled with self-doubt, thinking things like, "Oh my gosh. I can't do that because I'm going to have to go without certain types of food, and I'm going to end up not being able to eat the things I enjoy while everyone around me gets to eat cheeseburgers."

For just a minute, I want you to consider changing your thinking about food, nutrition and dieting. Approach what you eat in a different way. First, be kind to yourself. Food isn't like some addiction that you can just put aside, teetotal and be just fine. Because you're human, you're going to have to eat. Not only that, but deep down your body knows how much food it needs. It has the ability to signal to us that we need certain things and that we don't need others. That's why you might crave sugar or get heartburn after a trip to McDonald's. Now, you might be out of touch with these signals your body is sending you, so you're going to start by changing what you eat. It's the kind of calories that you consume that can make the most difference.

Start by adding in foods that can provide you with adequate nutrition that your body can't get anywhere else, such as leafy green vegetables, fruits and lean proteins. All those sound "healthy" and "diet-y," but they are also something else. They contain the vitamins, minerals and amino acids that your body needs to keep your cells operating at their optimal capacity. The food you consume is quite literally going to build your body. The adage "you are what you eat" is tried and true for a reason, and the best way to get the nutrients you need is by consuming foods that contain lots of them. I won't go into detail here because your doctor or health professional is the best person to consult about particulars. However, it is true for everyone that our body needs both fuel and building materials, so we want to support it by providing those as well as we can.

Then, consider this: You're putting things into your body that it doesn't need if you are busy eating fast food burgers and sodas, or if you're eating diet foods that have been processed to reduce calories/fat/sugar and thereby have had the nutrients stripped out of them. Your body can't really do much with refined sugar, white flour and overly processed proteins, but you're eating it so your body has to do something with it. If you are busy distracting your body and your appetite with these things, you're not leaving much room in your day or your stomach for the foods that can help make your body more efficient, more energetic and generally better able to do its job.

You Are What You Eat

I want you to take a look at specifically what you normally eat. Can you identify foods that are particularly useless in terms of nutritional value? Can you think of ways, small or large, that you could start adding in more nutritious foods or replacing those "empty" foods with useful, healthful foods?

Are there any foods that you just can't give up? Are there foods you enjoy but aren't currently a part of your diet?

I have several clients who have become great chefs. Susan was overweight and suffered from breast cancer. She beat the cancer but really wanted to lose weight. She studied multiple diets and came up with a menu of meals that are healthy, low in fat yet rich in proteins. She hosts family and friends every week. We love her food. She recently cooked spiralized zucchini with squash in a marinara sauce. Oh my, it was good.

Now, using a meal planner, develop your own personal strategy for changing your eating habits for the better. Keeping in mind your Physical Why will be helpful as you write because it can motivate you as you think about possible changes.

The Boiler Room

Most of us cringe a little when we hear the word "exercise." It conjures up images of being sweaty and out of breath at a gym where the rest of the people are fit, toned and barely perspiring. It sounds, frankly, like something that's a chore, something we have to do, not something we'd do for fun and not something that feels good.

In the boiler room of a ship, there is the constant movement of people (I envision the big, burly, sweaty men from the movie Titanic) shoveling coal into the furnaces so that the ship can move and get to where it's going. The fuel isn't interesting, just big piles of coal, but the human element in this equation, the visual I want you to have here, is that of those men in near-perpetual motion, working hard to keep the ship running on time to reach its destination.

Just like your body needs the fuel (and thank goodness that food is more interesting than coal!), it needs movement to keep on track to reach its goal. I'd like you to take a second and consider that rather than "exercising" we should start just by moving. Not with some sense of competition or with an end result in sight (at first, or even ever) but rather with the intention to get to know your body by moving it in ways that are pleasing. It's so easy, especially as we continue to become a more computer-centered society, to stop moving, to just sit in a chair all day sending emails and enter data into spreadsheets. If we were computers ourselves, this would be fine, but we're flesh-and-bone bodies that atrophy from lack of movement.

I Like the Way You Move

Instead of dwelling on exercise, I want you to simply think about movement for now. For this journal, consider ways that you have liked to move in the past. Did you used to play rec basketball? Did you walk to class when you were in school? Did you love the monkey bars as a kid?

What kinds of movement do you already engage in? Are there specific ways you want to move but are restricted by your body at the moment? How do you feel when you move? Do you feel stiff and sore? What kinds of movement do you know you like right now? Do you take pleasure in stretching or walking? Do you like to sweat?

Can you think of ways now to bring more movement into your daily life? This might mean something like taking a walk during your lunch hour, standing and walking along the sidelines at your kids' soccer games, taking a yoga class or joining an adult sports league.

Of course, before you introduce any new strenuous activity into your life, you should consult your doctor to make sure it's right for you, but considering these kinds of changes now will prepare you to ask those questions.

Recharging Station

The third component to this section is getting good, quality, consistent sleep. I can hear you groaning now, "But, John, I don't have time to sleep. I have too many bills to pay, too much work and too many things I want to accomplish! Didn't you just spend a bunch of time telling me to pursue my passions, save money and add more movement into my day? Now, you're telling me to get more sleep?"

Yes, I am. The long and the short of it is that without adequate, quality sleep, you will be hard-pressed to accomplish any of your other goals.

We as a society have been conditioned to regard sleep as a luxury, a waste of time or even a sign of weakness of character or a lack of willpower, but poor sleep has been medically proven to coincide with colds/flu, unhealthy skin, weight gain, diabetes, heart disease, cancer, stress, anxiety and depression. If you think that giving up sleep is going to help you make gains in other areas, you'll find that the results are short-lived and, frankly, not worth the sacrifice.

Figuring out what the best sleep strategy is for your body and lifestyle is best left up to you and a medical professional, but I can guarantee that most of us need more sleep or better sleep.

First, you need to make sleep a priority. Time-block in sleep if you have to, just find a way to get the rest you need. Next, make sure that your bedroom is set up for sleep. Don't set up your home office in your bedroom. Remove the TV, and make the bed as comfortable and inviting as possible. Then, develop a bedtime routine that encourages feelings of comfort and relaxation: Softly light the room, turn off your phone and enjoy a mug of herbal tea. Make getting ready for sleep a routine that helps signal to your body that it is time for rest.

The Land of Nod

Sleep can feel like a guilty pleasure, especially if you've been depriving yourself of adequate rest for a long time now. I'd like you to think about what you like about sleep, and what kinds of things help you sleep.

What things currently keep you from getting enough sleep? Are these things priorities? If you were better rested, happier or less stressed, would you be better able to deal with the big "rocks" in your daily schedule?

Describe your ideal bedtime routine and brainstorm ways to implement it now.

Start Small

You're going to start small. A lot of times people will get really hyped up, ready to make big changes and say, "I want to run a mile" or "I want to lose 50 pounds." Well, that's great, and those are great goals to have. But don't expect to go out tomorrow, if you haven't ever run before, and run a mile. You're going to have to start with running to the end of the block, and from there you've got to run to the next block. Keep that big goal in mind. Write it down, but also set smaller goals. Start with some that are very easily achievable. Start by running to the end of the block for a week or two weeks. Then, run to the next block for a couple weeks.

Starting small will allow you to kind of trick yourself into continuing toward your bigger goal because we humans love to be rewarded. We love to be told we've done a good job. Set goals that you can achieve immediately so you don't get burnt out on your way to the top.

Small Is Beautiful

Write down three goals — one nutritional goal, one activity goal and one sleep goal — that you would like to realize in the next 30 days.

Why are these three goals important to you? What can you do to ensure that you achieve them? Do you foresee any obstacles standing between you and realizing these goals?

Think back to your Physical Why. Do these goals reflect that?

Stay Well

We can easily get discouraged as we go through our day-to-day life. For example, some emergency arises and we don't get our run in, or a meeting runs long and we end up grabbing a fast food burger for lunch. It can be even more discouraging when we find ourselves sick. Having to lie in bed and drink lots of fluids not only gets in the way of the necessities like laundry and making dinner, but it can make us feel like we're not making progress toward our goals.

Throughout this process, it is important that you take care of your body and be kind to yourself. Let yourself have the rest you need to do the hard work of bringing balance into your life. If you get sick, allow yourself the time that you need to get well, and see a doctor so you have all the tools and information you need to recover.

Taking a daily vitamin isn't a bad idea, and neither is making sure you get your flu shot. (Consult your doctor on this, of course.)

More than anything, though, continue to treat yourself as you would your best friend. Give yourself understanding and respect. This will afford you the greatest amount of wellness as you pursue your goals.

As we wrap up this area of the book, I want to hit you with some rapid-fire resources, ideas and tips to help you along in pursuit of your goals. Some tips you'll be able to apply to all areas of your life, because motivating yourself along your journey to balance looks the same whether you're thinking about money or exercise.

Give Yourself a Break

Changing a habit takes 21 to 30 days. They say it takes 21 days if you do it every single day exactly the same way. Most of us can't do that, so when you set your mind to changing a habit (giving up smoking, adding more movement to your day or eating more leafy greens) give yourself 30 days to change. Anytime you try to incorporate a new habit into your life you need time to let it sink in. It's going to take three to four weeks, so give yourself permission to take that time.

Take a Deep Breath

Deep breathing is a simple yet powerful way to increase your energy and your health. Every so often just take a big, giant deep breath. In through your nose and out through your mouth. Do it three times. Deep breathing clears the mind, clears the soul, clears the body and helps with energy and health.

Positive Visualization

I want to touch again on something we covered in the introduction to the book, and that is about how to be a friend to yourself. Positive self-talk is critical to your success, especially in the Physical Area. Don't beat yourself up. We talk to ourselves all day long, and especially when we're exercising or eating, these thoughts directly affect the way we experience things. On average, a person has around 60,000 thoughts a day. Work to make the majority of those thoughts, or at least half, positive, affirming thoughts. This is a realizable goal, because all you have to do to reach that halfway point is to counter half of those negative thoughts with positive ones.

Spend time mindfully encouraging yourself. Use positive mantras. Say, "I am fit. I am positive. I am strong." One of mine that I say when I'm running is "Strong and skinny. I'm strong and skinny." "I love and approve of myself." Fill your mind with images of things that are lovely or divine, a great story, something with hope and good humor. Positive visualization will lift your spirit and settle your soul.

Laws of Attraction

It is remarkable to watch the laws of attraction at work. You can make these laws work for you. Like attracts like. By focusing on positive or negative thoughts, a person brings positive or negative experiences into their life. This is another way to say, what comes around goes around. If you do bad, bad will come back to you. The laws of attraction work up to the second in synchronized connection with other people and nature. Thoughts are running around in people's heads all the time. You may be thinking the exact same thing at the same time as someone else in another part of the country. You may actually call a friend at exactly the same time the friend is contacting you. These positive or negative energies are operating at all times in the universe. Be a part of the positive, the uplifting, the inspirational. Joshua Warren, in "Use the Force: A Jedi's Guide to the Law of Attraction," explains that we must learn how to train our minds to hone in on our intention; enhance our connection to the universe; and ensure that our actions, words and thoughts are in harmony with accomplishing our goals.

Reach Out to Others

Staying positive and committed is much easier if you have others you can rely on to keep you accountable. If you keep all of your goals to yourself, you're going to be less likely to commit to keeping them. There is great power in the presence of a support system. You can also join or form a group. If I were not part of workout groups and I didn't tell people I was going to be there, I know myself, and I know that I would not show up. Creating or joining a group creates accountability and support. There are lots of places to do this, such as your neighborhood, your workplace and your church, and you can find more by checking out websites like Meetup.com.

Start Wherever You Are

We all start somewhere. That sounds pretty simplistic, but it really is the truth. We're all starting somewhere, and where you're starting in your life's script, in your story, in how you got to where you are is perfectly fine. It is your history, your path, your life, your story and your filter. We all got here, and we all start somewhere. The best time to plant the tree was 40 years ago. The second best time is today.

We can't erase the past. We can't change what happened in the past, but we can definitely change where we're going. Lou Holtz, a college football coach, said, "I'm not who I want to be, I'm not who I'm going to be, but thank God I'm not who I used to be." Wherever you're starting, whoever you are today, it's OK; it's great. It's your story. Embrace your story, but start working to make that story what you want it to be. If you want to make a change, make a change.

Run Your Own Race

This journey is not anybody else's journey. You're not competing against anybody. You're not trying to beat somebody. You're trying to get yourself a little more active and a little bit more nutritionally sound so that you are as prepared as you can be to take care of your finances, figure out what your unique ability is and achieve that balance you desire.

What's more, ignore the spectators. They're not the ones doing the hard, sweaty, inelegant work of running your race. You are.

Don't Give Up

Don't give up. No matter what you do, keep plugging away. You're going to have setbacks; you're going to slip. Just don't give up. Resolve anew every morning to keep plugging along and to do the best you can. Your life will improve; you will achieve greater levels of balance and fulfillment. Just don't give up.

R.U. Darby was a businessman in the early 20th century who had hoped to become rich by finding gold. He found a vein of gold, but eventually the vein disappeared. He and his team drilled on desperately hoping to find the vein of gold again. They tried, but did not find it. So they quit. Darby sold the equipment to a junk collector. The junk man hired an engineer, who determined the previous owner did not understand fault lines in the area. He calculated the vein picked up again three feet from where the previous miner had stopped digging. This is exactly where it was found. Darby was only three feet from success. This is another reason to never give up.

Darby learned a valuable lesson. He went on to become one of the nation's top sellers of life insurance.

"I stopped three feet from gold, but I will never stop because men say 'no' when I ask them to buy insurance," he told Napoleon Hill in Hill's famous book, "Think and Grow Rich."

In the case of Julie Moss, she was only 30 yards from success. She could have stopped running the Ironman. Instead, she crawled to the finish line.

"Most great people have attained their greatest success just one step beyond their greatest failure," said Napoleon Hill.

Carpe Diem

The enlightened lifestyle combines wealth, health and happiness to achieve a well-rounded and balanced life. Having a solid financial strategy, a good diet and exercise lifestyle and a passion for doing something you love — all are achievable, the rewards bountiful.

We know money alone cannot buy happiness, but lack of money can cause unhappiness.

As we get older, change comes to us. If we can anticipate the challenge ahead, we can prepare for it. A successful retirement is not achieved at a moment's notice.

At the top of Abraham Maslow's hierarchy of needs is self-actualization, a state of full creativity and use of your talents. At the lower levels, one must first achieve safety, a sense of love and belonging and self-esteem. If you are constantly worried about your finances, you won't reach higher levels of living. That is why it is critical to have a financial strategy. With your mind and body at peace, you can pursue a path that allows you to become the best person that you can be.

Surround yourself with people who love you and support you. Align yourself with mentors who really have your best interests at heart.

Dr. Karl Menninger, co-founder of The Menninger Clinic, worked with extremely difficult mentally ill patients. He wrote,

"Not infrequently, we observe that a patient who is in a phase of recovery from what may have been a rather long illness shows continued improvement, past the point of his former 'normal' state of existence. He not only gets well, to use the vernacular; he gets as well as he was, and then continues to improve still further. He increases his productivity; he expands his life and its horizons. He develops new talents, new powers, new effectiveness. He becomes, one might say, 'weller than well.'"

The fact that a person with a severe mental illness can achieve a state of superior wellness speaks volumes about human potential. What is achievable for you and me?!!

By executing a well-thought-out plan of action, a person can reach new heights of productivity, gain deeper insights and meaning and grow to higher levels of love, experience and compassion. Your joy will become contagious and perhaps lift up a neighbor, friend or family member.

Thank you for reading this book. I hope you have found some good ideas to implement in your life. Now seize the day. Time is of the essence.

John J. Navin is a financial advisor with two decades of experience in retirement planning, insurance, wealth management and helping others pursue their goals.

John has passed the Series 65 and 66 securities exams and is a licensed insurance producer in six states. He is a Registered Investment Adviser.

John lives in Nashville, Tennessee, with his wife, Dana. He has two beautiful daughters, Kailey and Julia.

John is an active member of his community, serving as a member of both the Williamson County Chamber of Commerce and the Nashville Entrepreneur Center. Outside of work, he enjoys traveling, hunting, biking, swimming and gardening. In recent years, John has run marathons and triathlons, and, in 2011, earned the prestigious title of Ironman, completing Ironman Wisconsin; in 2016, he completed Ironman Lake Placid in New York.

His strengths lie in connecting with people, and providing the possibilities for his clients to spend more time doing what they love, living their life with meaning and passion, and pursuing dreams that become a reality with a solid financial strategy.

Combined with his real-life experiences, fitness expertise and his love of finance, John offers a holistic approach toward financial planning and living.

www.ingramcontent.com/pod-product-compliance
Lightning Source LLC
Chambersburg PA
CBHW070050210526
45170CB00012B/634